Big-Note Piano

2ND EDITION

THE IRISH SONGBOOK

ISBN 978-0-7935-7572-5

HAL•LEONARD®
CORPORATION
7777 W. BLUEMOUND RD. P.O. BOX 13819 MILWAUKEE, WI 53213

In Australia Contact:
Hal Leonard Australia Pty. Ltd.
4 Lentara Court
Cheltenham, Victoria, 3192 Australia
Email: ausadmin@halleonard.com.au

Visit Hal Leonard Online at
www.halleonard.com

BELIEVE ME, IF ALL THOSE ENDEARING YOUNG CHARMS

Words and Music by
THOMAS MOORE

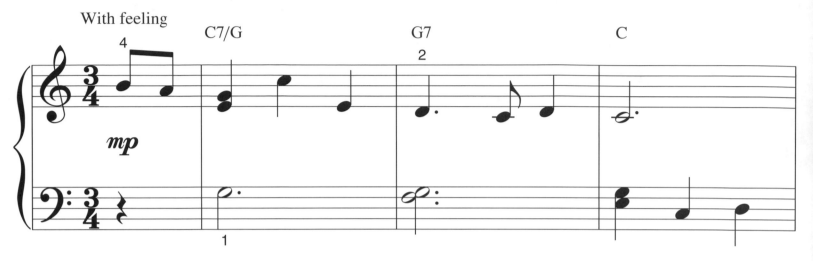

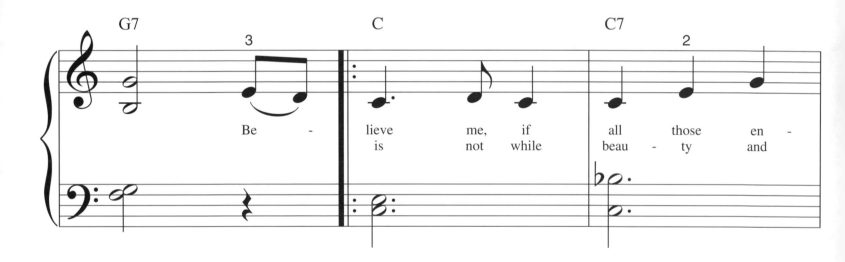

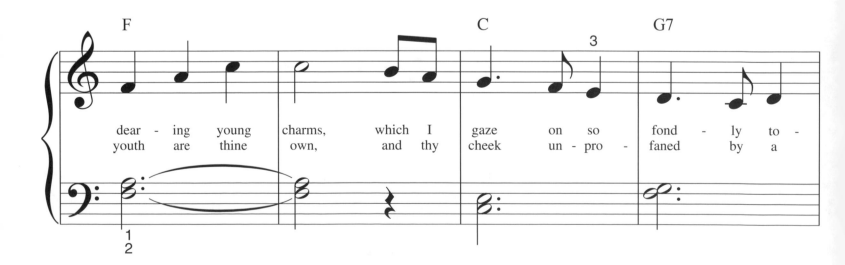

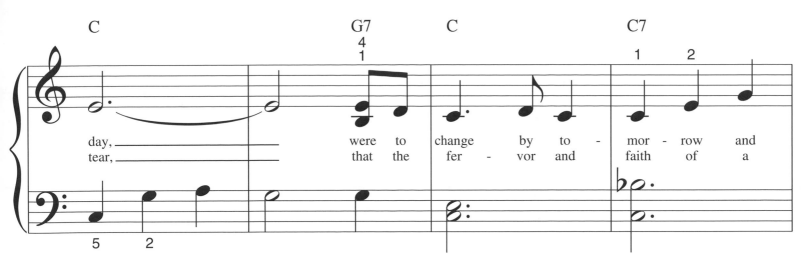

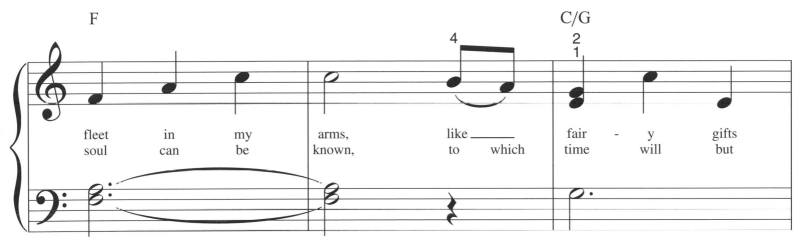

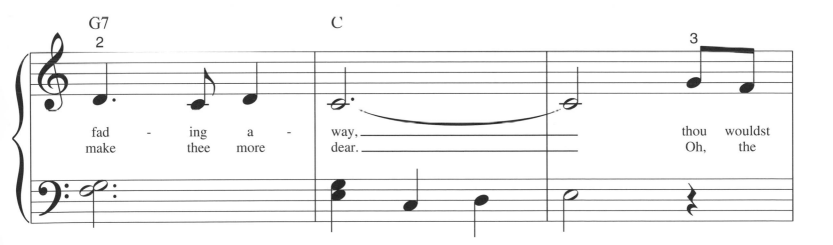

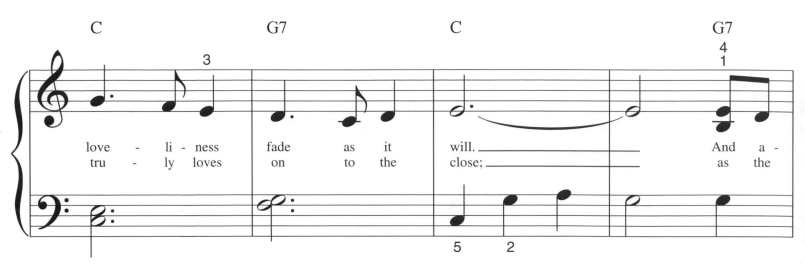

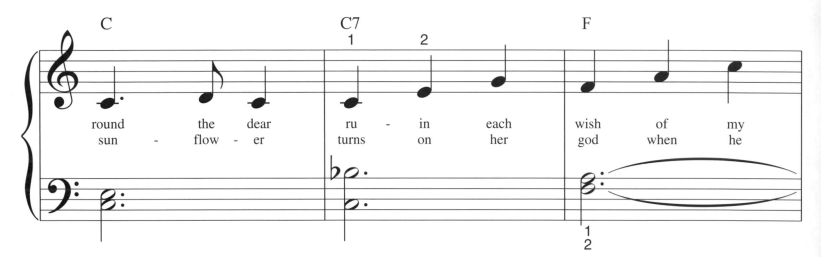

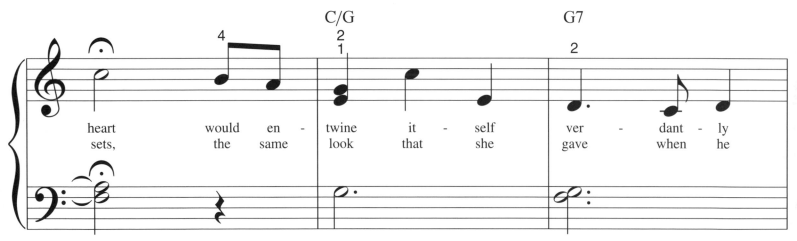

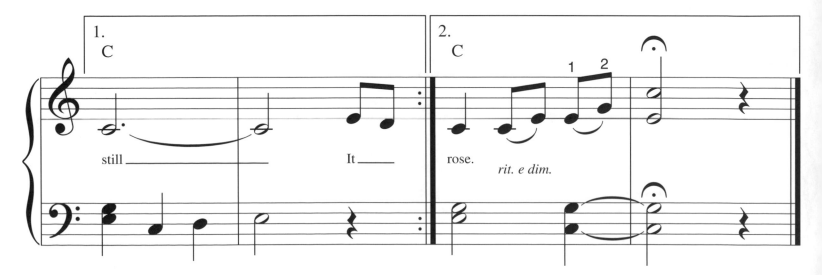

DANNY BOY

Words by FREDERICK EDWARD WEATHERLY
Traditional Irish Folk Melody

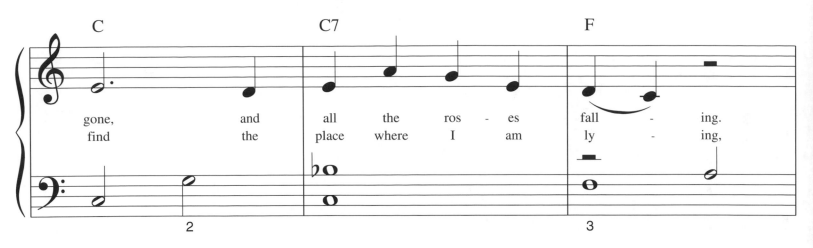

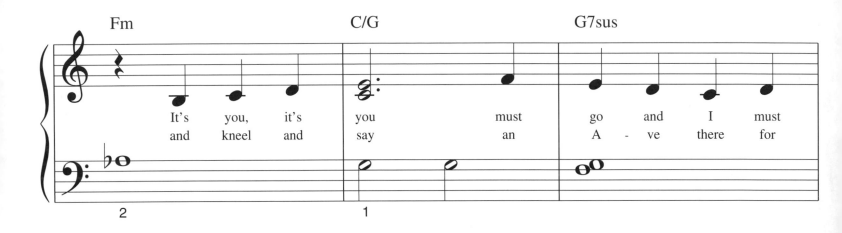

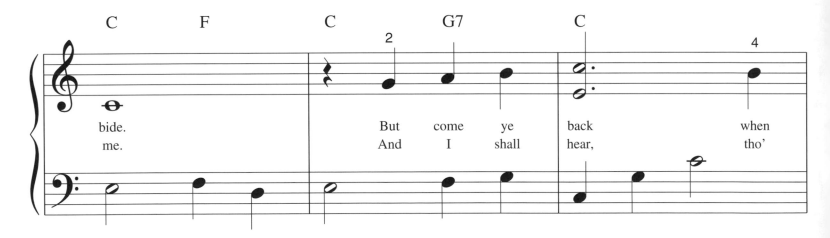

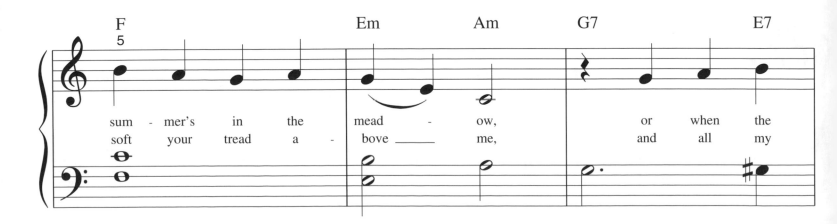

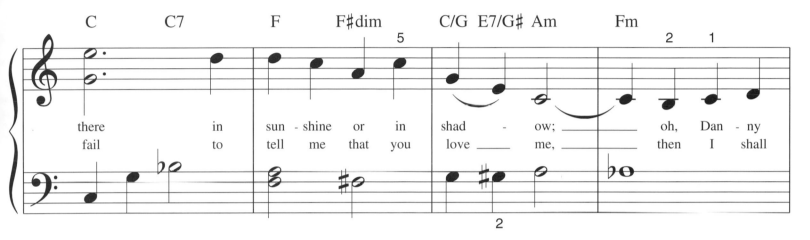

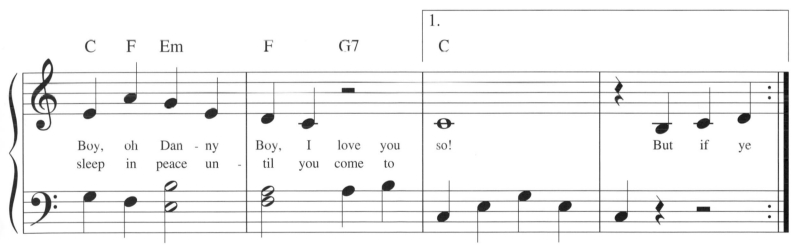

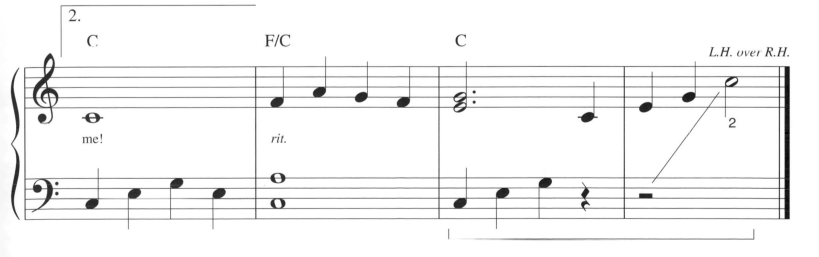

THE GALWAY PIPER

Irish Folksong

Lightly

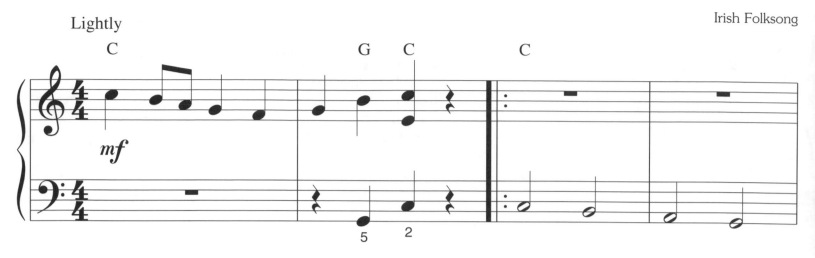

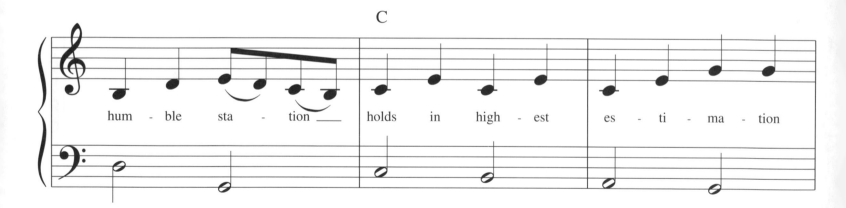

1. Ev - 'ry per - son in the na - tion or of great or
2., 3. *See additional lyrics*

hum - ble sta - tion holds in high - est es - ti - ma - tion

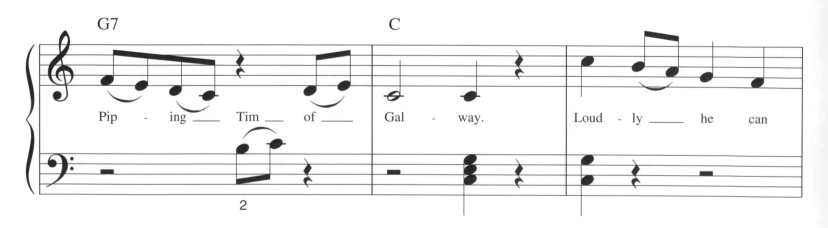

Pip - ing Tim of Gal - way. Loud - ly he can

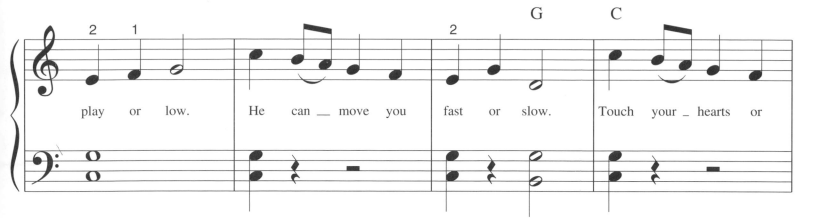

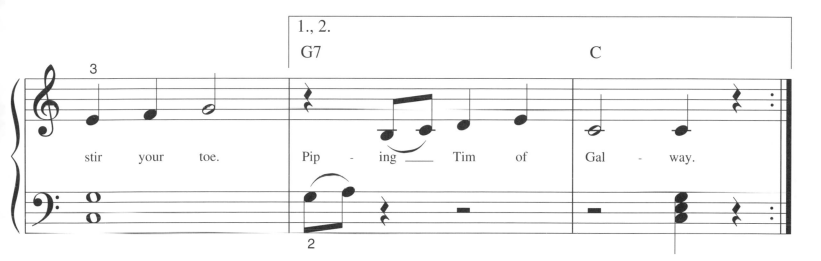

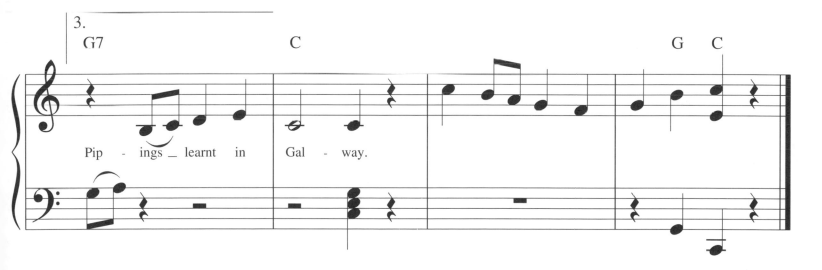

Additional Lyrics

2. When the wedding bells are ringing,
   His the breath that stirs the singing.
   Then in jigs the folks go swinging.
   What a splendid piper!
   He will blow from eve to morn,
   Counting sleep a thing of scorn,
   Old is he, but not outworn.
   Know you such a piper?

3. When he walks the highway pealing,
   'Round his head the birds come wheeling.
   Tim has carols worth the stealing,
   Piping Tim of Galway.
   Thrush and linnet, finch and lark
   To each other twitter "Hark!"
   Soon they sing from light to dark
   Pipings learnt in Galway.

GARRYOWEN

Irish Folksong

Quickly

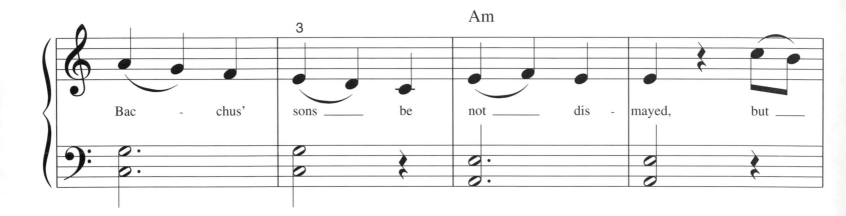

1. Let _____
2.-5. *See additional lyrics*

Bac - chus' sons _____ be not _____ dis - mayed, but _____

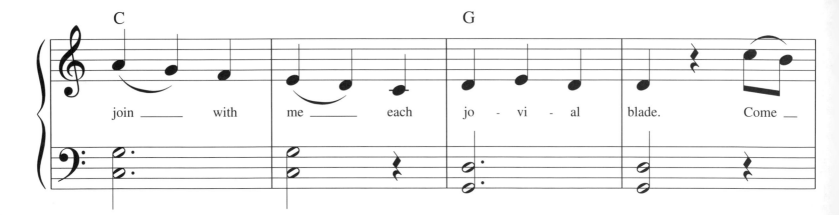

join _____ with me _____ each jo - vi - al blade. Come _____

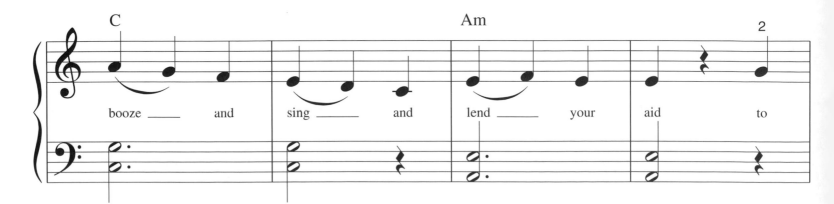

booze _____ and sing _____ and lend _____ your aid to

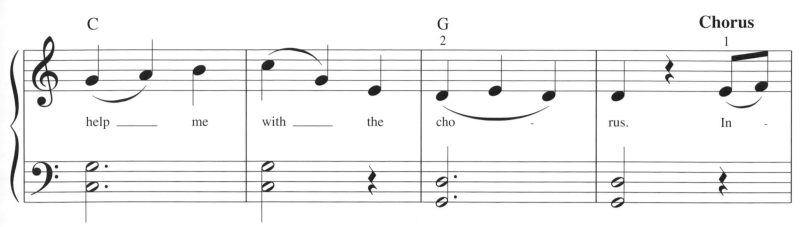

C   G   **Chorus**

help _____ me   with _____ the   cho -   rus.   In -

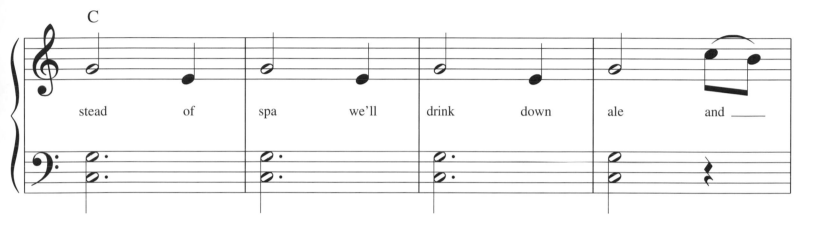

C

stead   of   spa   we'll   drink   down   ale   and _____

F

pay   the   reck - 'ning   on   the   nail.   No

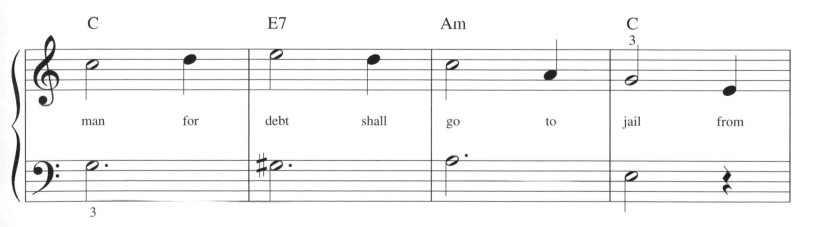

C   E7   Am   C

man   for   debt   shall   go   to   jail   from

12

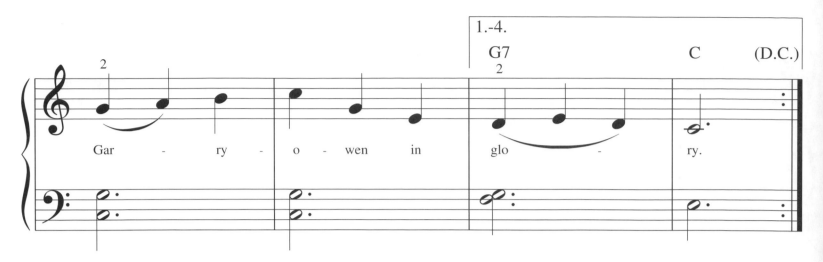

Gar - ry - o - wen in glo - ry.

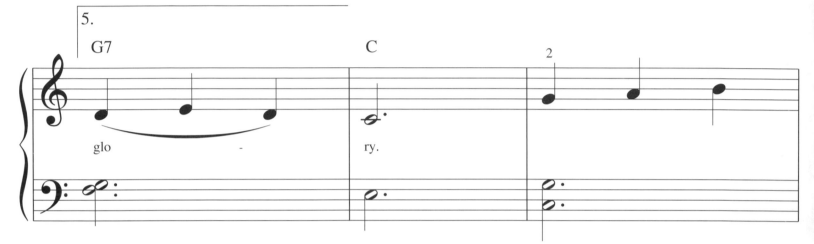

glo - ry.

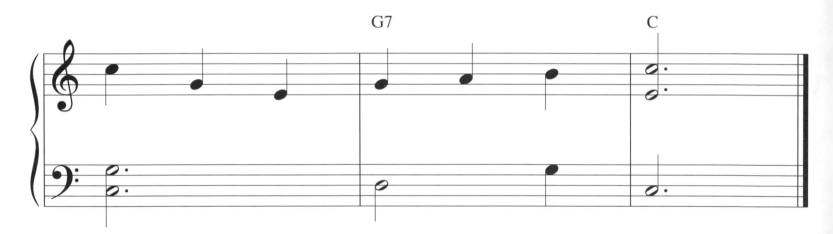

Additional Lyrics

2. We are the boys that take delight in
   Smashing the Limerick lights when lighting
   Through all the streets like sporters fighting
   And tearing all before us.
   Chorus

3. We'll break the windows, we'll break the doors,
   The watch knock down by threes and fours;
   Then let the doctors work their cures
   And tinker up our bruises.
   Chorus

4. We'll beat the bailiffs out of fun,
   We'll make the mayors and sheriffs run;
   We are the boys no man dares dun
   If he regards a whole skin.
   Chorus

5. Our hearts so stout have got us fame,
   For soon 'tis known from whence we came;
   Where'er we go they dread the name
   Of Garryowen in glory.
   Chorus

GIRL I LEFT BEHIND ME

Traditional Irish

With spirit

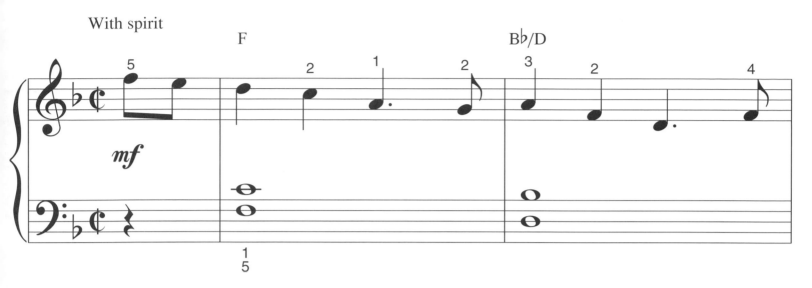

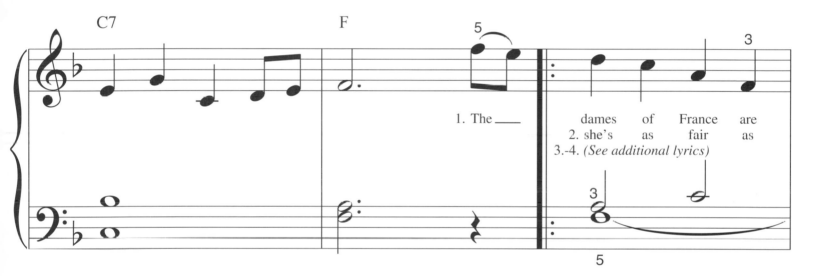

1. The _____ dames of France are
2. she's as fair as
3.-4. *(See additional lyrics)*

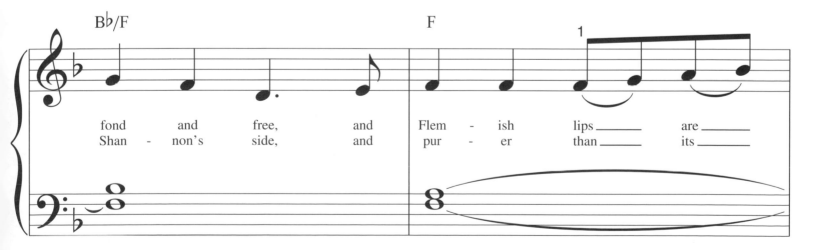

fond and free, and
Shan - non's side, and
Flem - ish lips _____ are _____
pur - er than _____ its _____

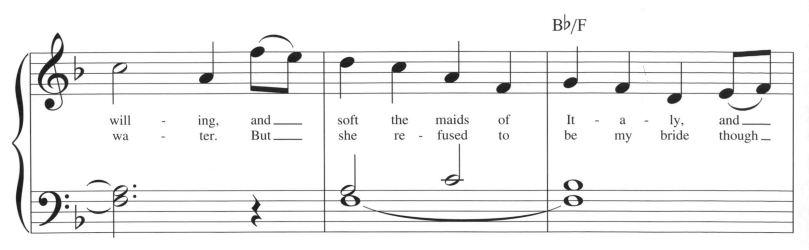

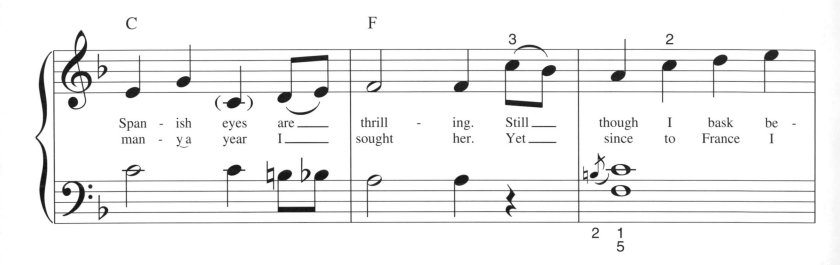

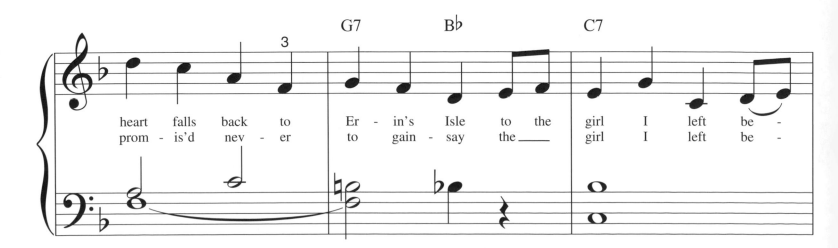

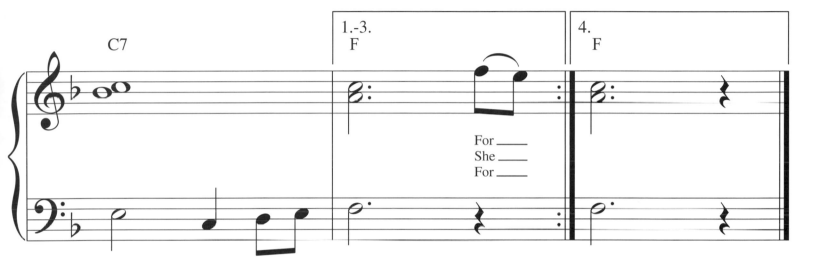

Additional Lyrics

3. She says, "My own dear love, come home,
    My friends are rich and many;
    Or else abroad with you I'll roam,
    A soldier stout as any.
    If you'll not come, nor let me go,
    I'll think you have resigned me."
    My heart nigh broke when I answered "no"
    To the girl I left behind me.

4. For never shall my true love brave
    A life of war and toiling,
    And never as a skulking slave
    I'll tread my native soil on.
    But were it free or to be freed,
    The battle's close would find me
    To Ireland bound, nor message need
    From the girl I left behind me.

HARRIGAN

Words and Music by
GEORGE M. COHAN

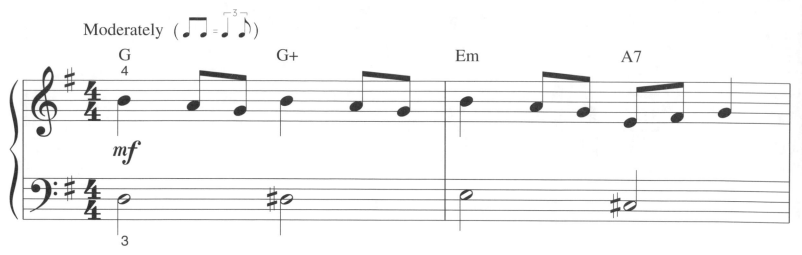

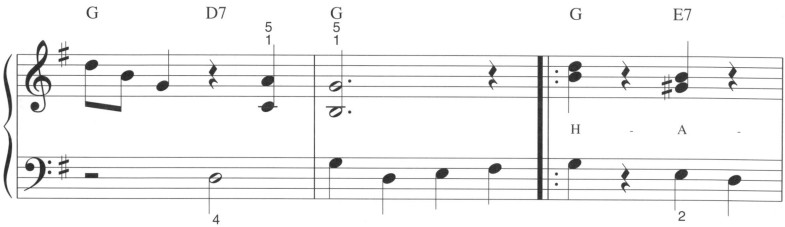

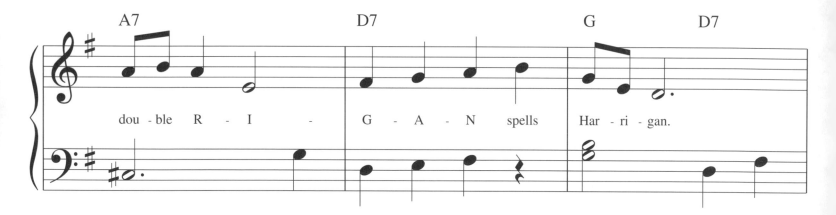

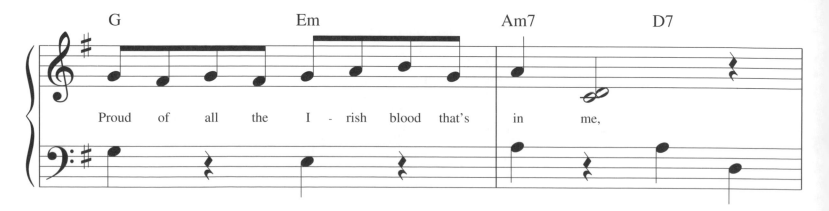

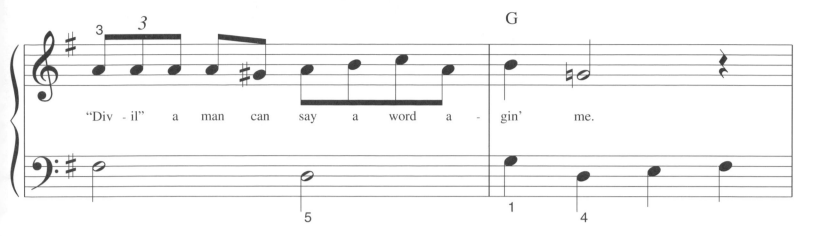

"Div - il" a man can say a word a - gin' me.

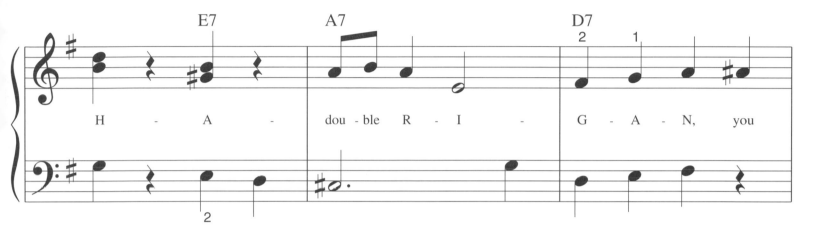

H - A - dou-ble R - I - G - A - N, you

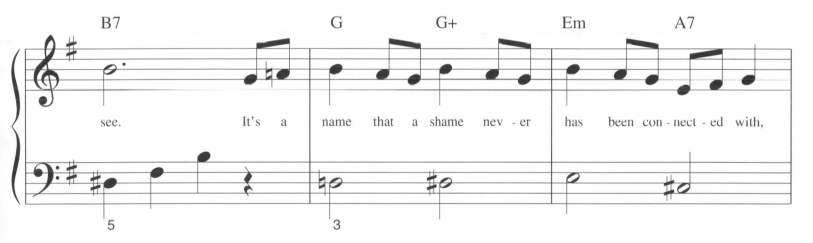

see.   It's a name that a shame nev-er   has been con-nect-ed with,

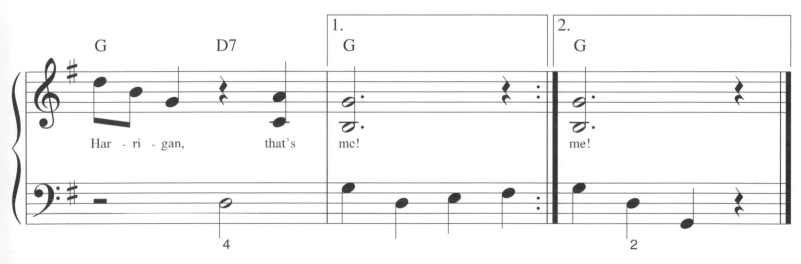

Har - ri - gan,   that's   me!   me!

HAS ANYBODY HERE SEEN KELLY?

Words and Music by C.W. MURPHY,
WILL LETTERS and WILLIAM J. McKENNA

Moderately

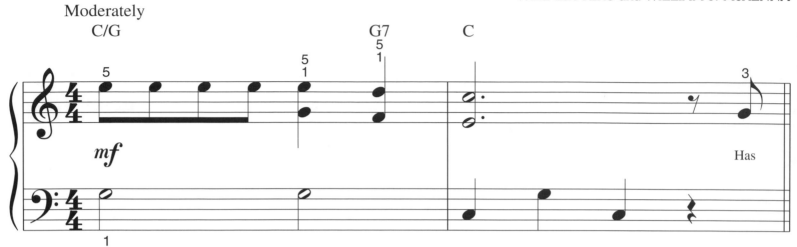

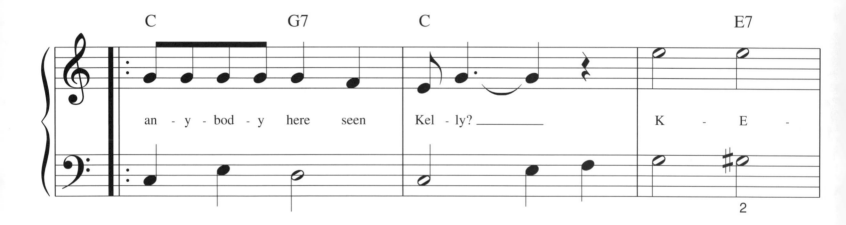

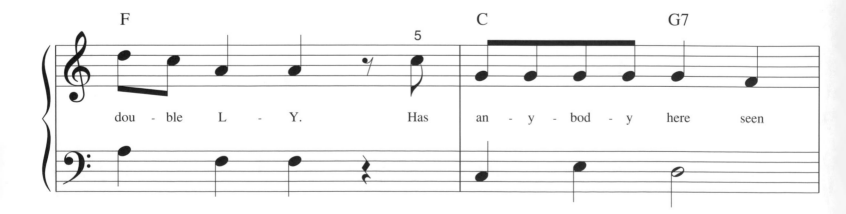

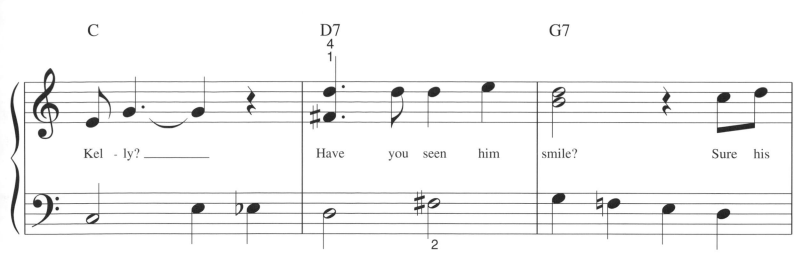

Kel - ly? _____ Have you seen him smile? Sure his

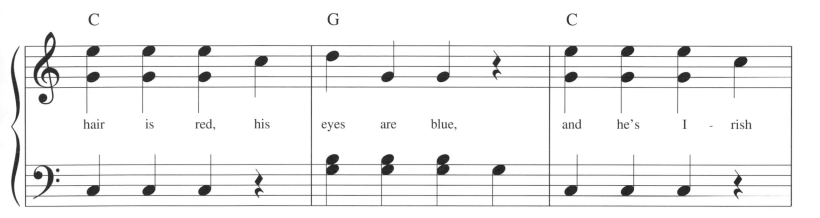

hair is red, his eyes are blue, and he's I - rish

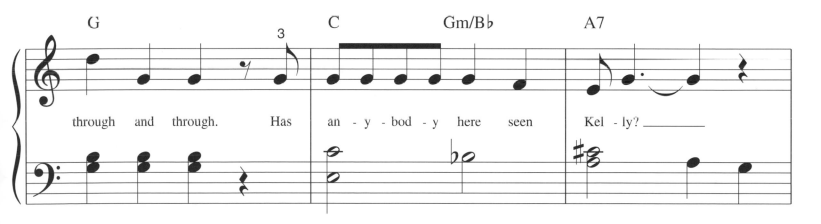

through and through. Has an - y - bod - y here seen Kel - ly? _____

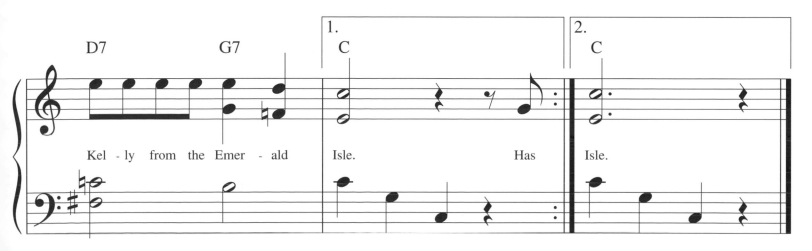

Kel - ly from the Emer - ald Isle. Has Isle.

I'LL TAKE YOU HOME AGAIN, KATHLEEN

Words and Music by
THOMAS WESTENDORF

Slowly

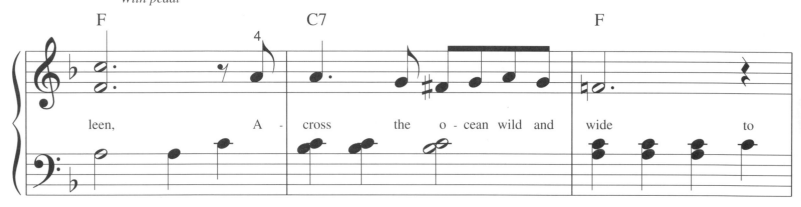

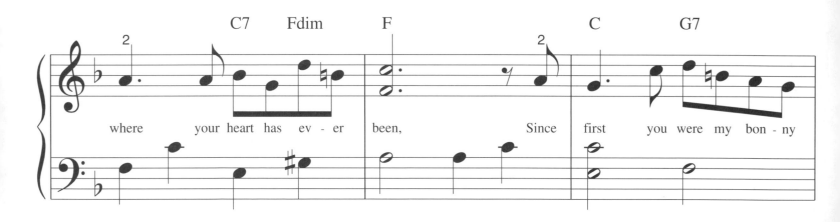

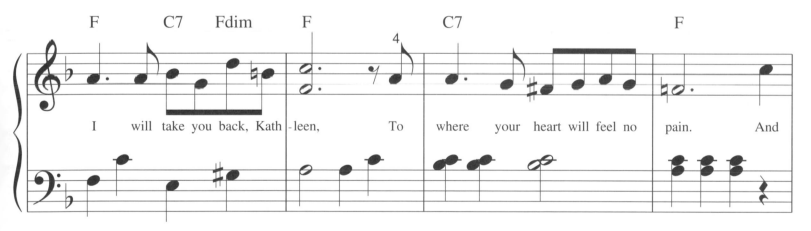

IF I KNOCK THE 'L' OUT OF KELLY

Words by SAM M. LEWIS and JOE YOUNG
Music by BERT GRANT

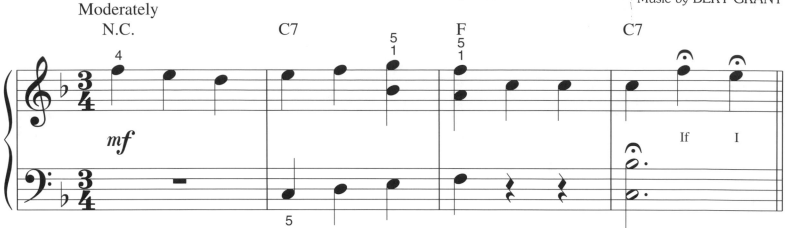

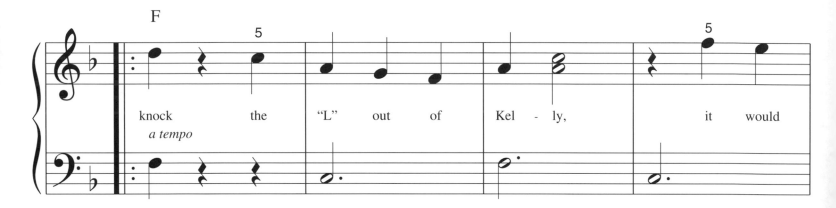

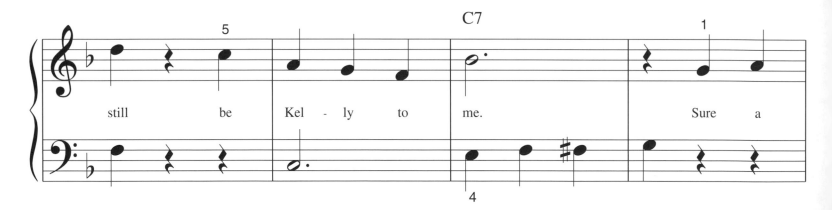

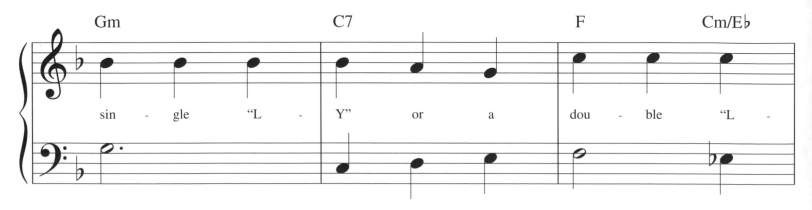

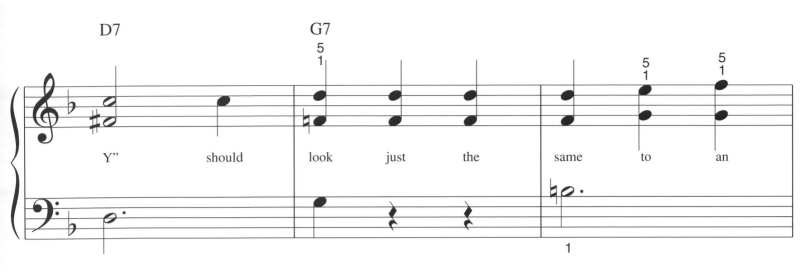

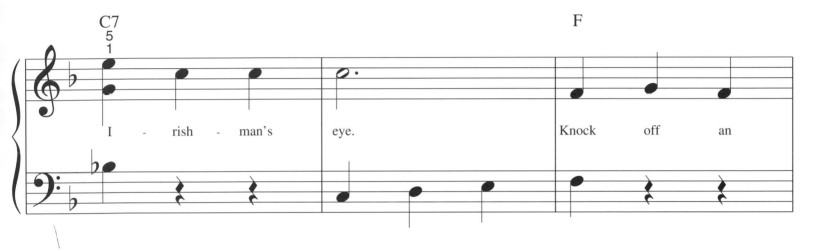

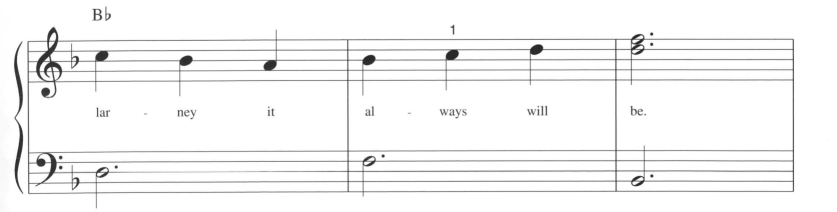

23

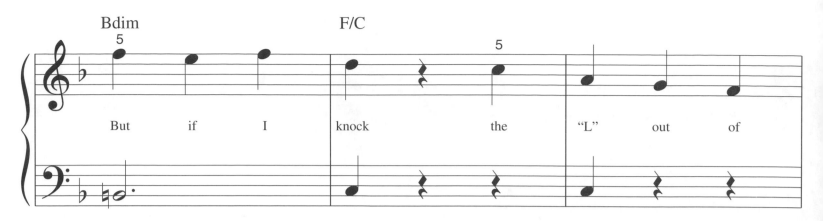

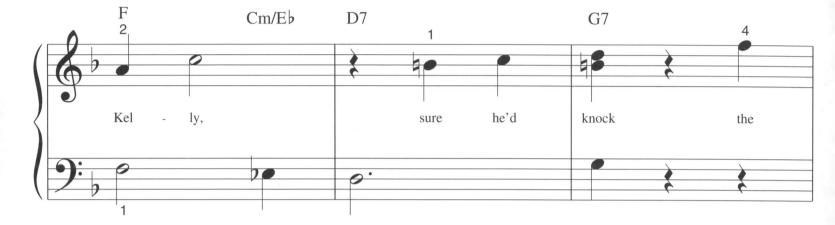

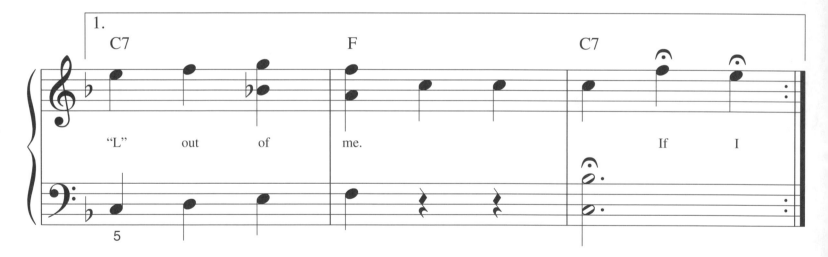

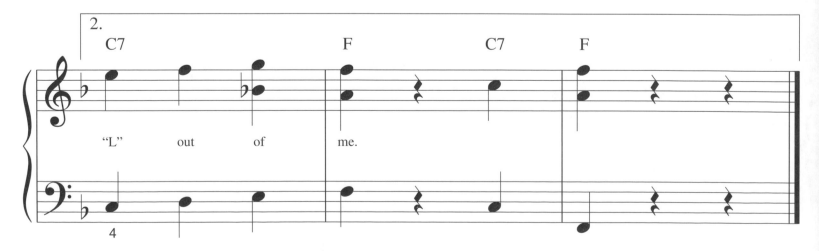

THE IRISH WASHERWOMAN

Irish Folksong

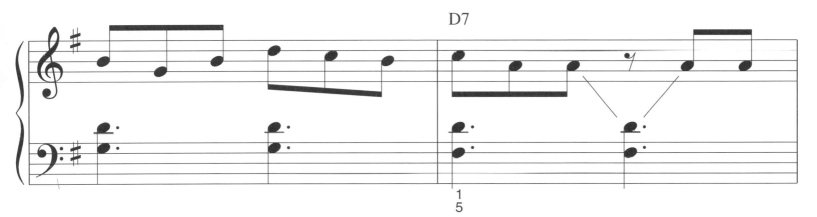

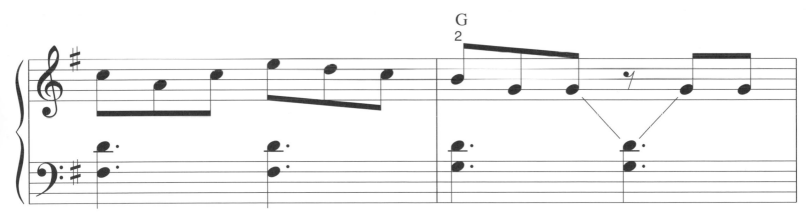

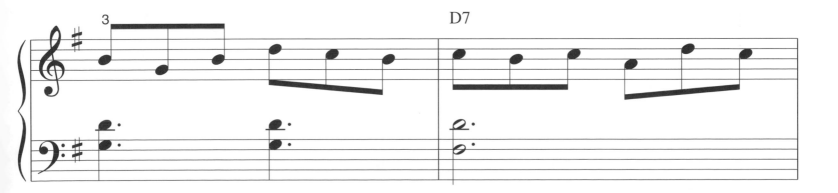

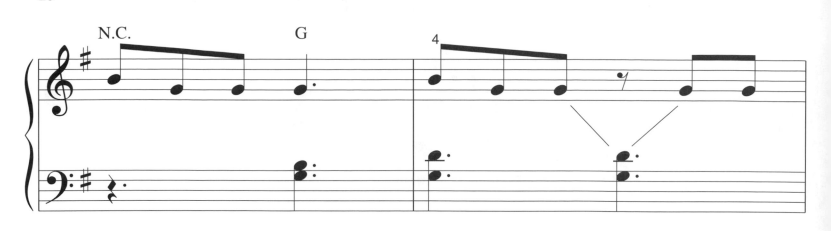

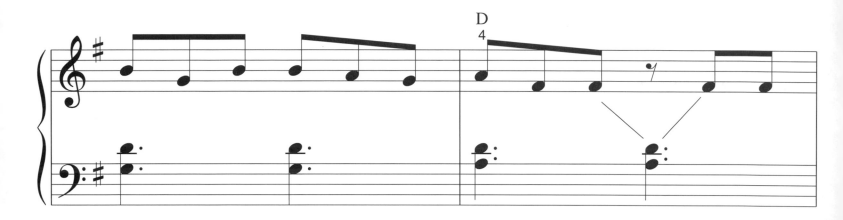

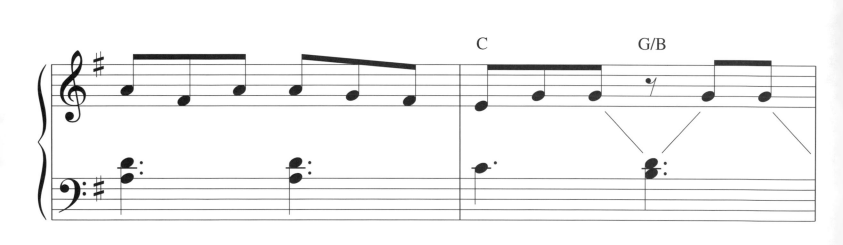

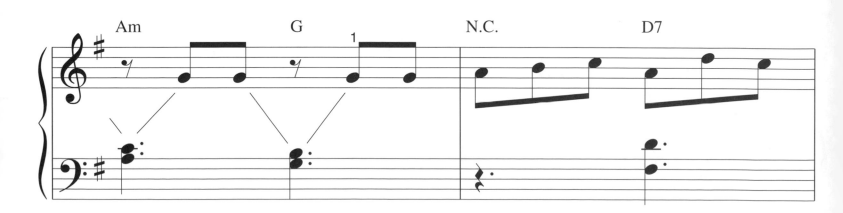

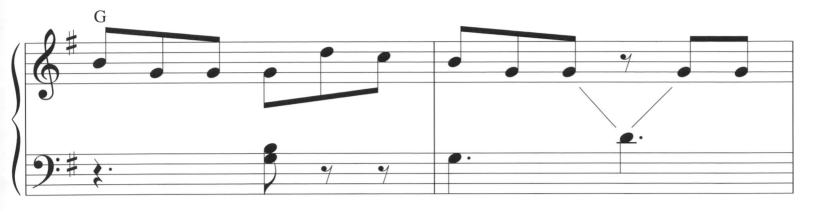

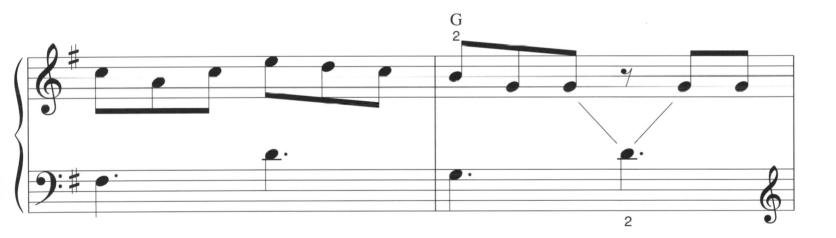

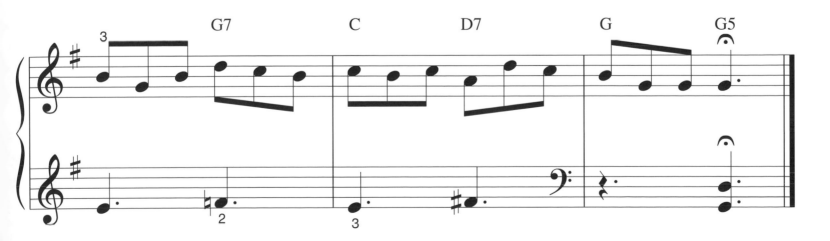

KERRY DANCE

By J.L. MOLLOY

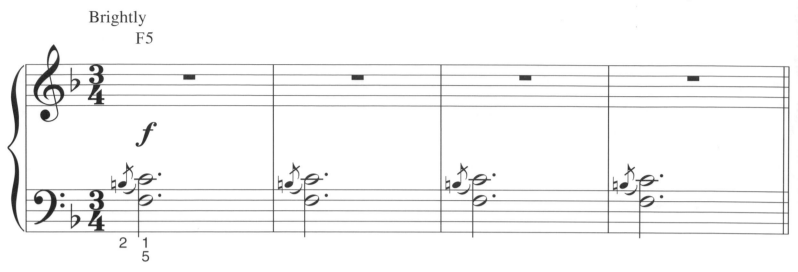

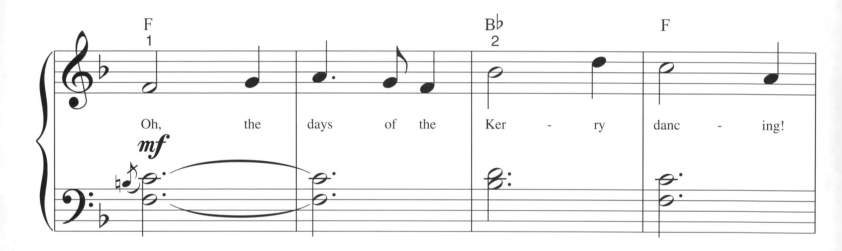

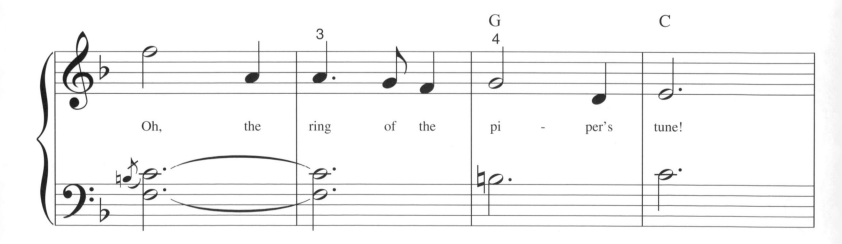

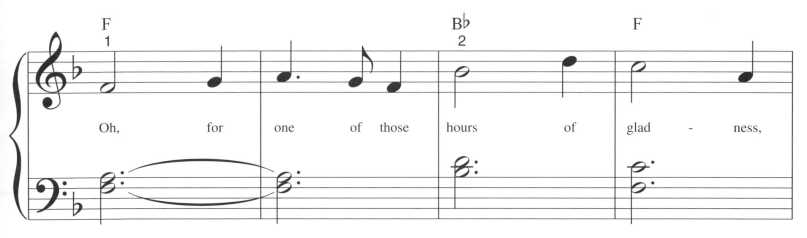

Oh, for one of those hours of glad - ness,

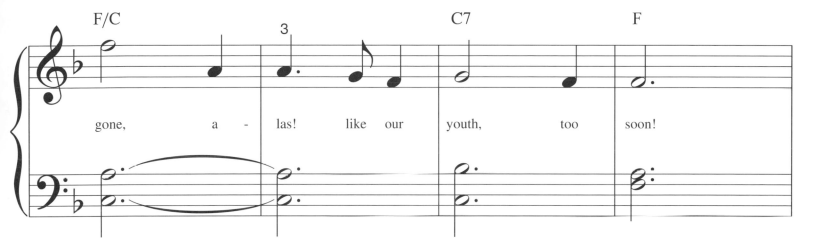

gone, a - las! like our youth, too soon!

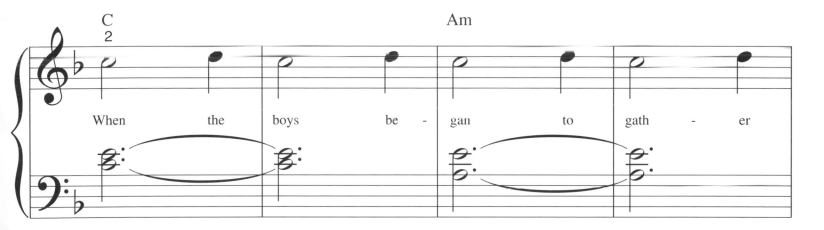

When the boys be - gan to gath - er

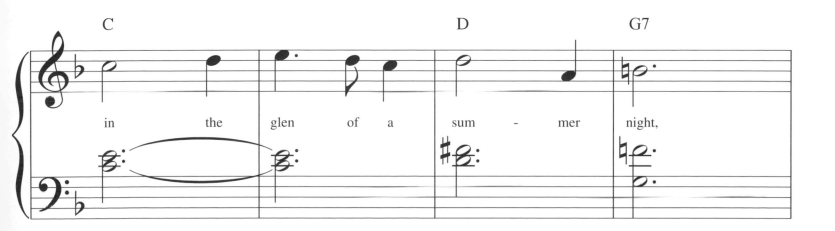

in the glen of a sum - mer night,

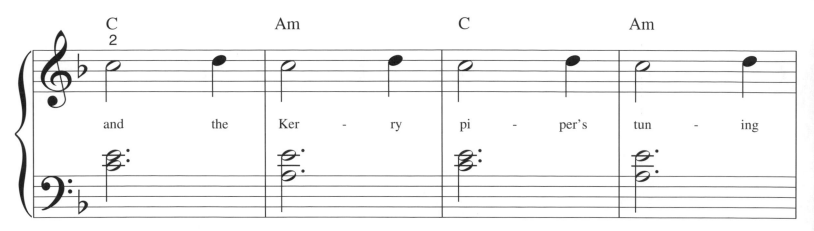

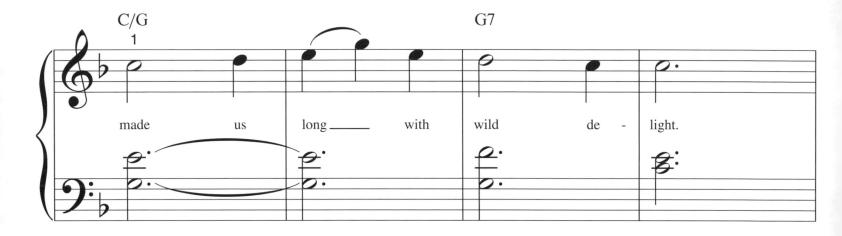

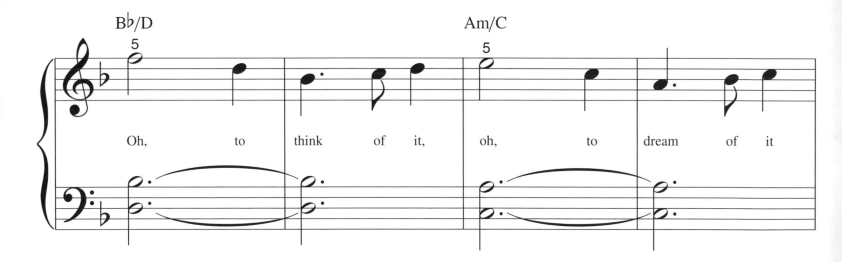

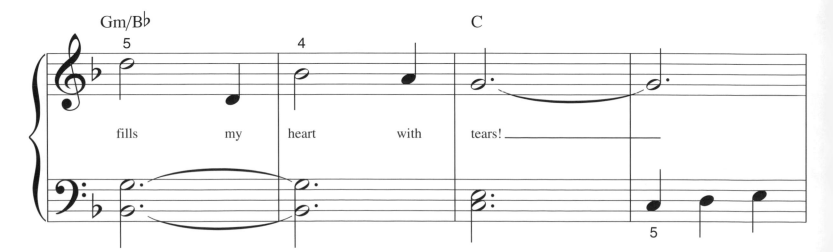

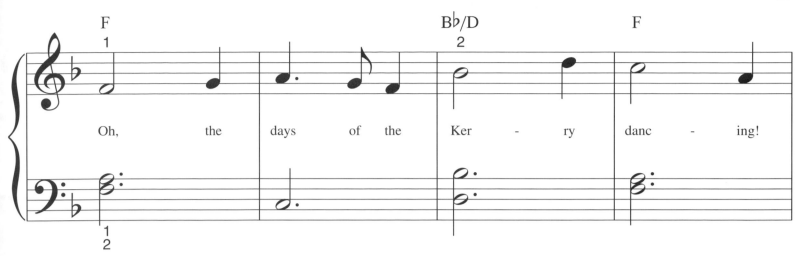

Oh, the days of the Ker - ry danc - ing!

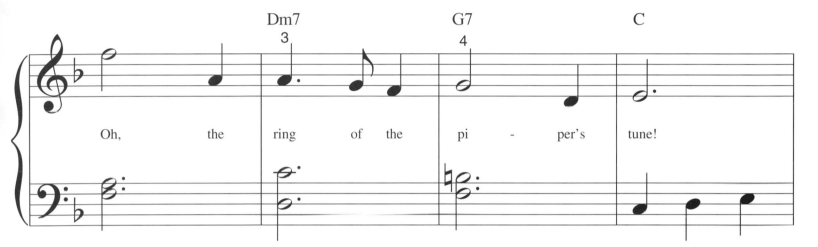

Oh, the ring of the pi - per's tune!

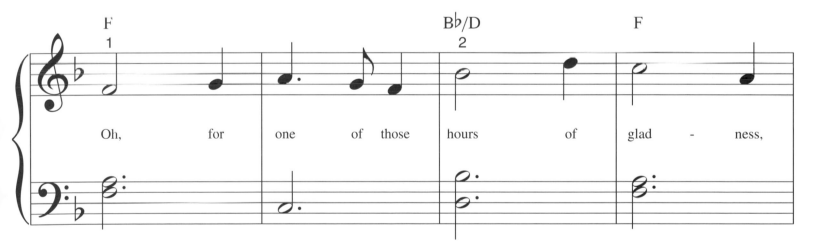

Oh, for one of those hours of glad - ness,

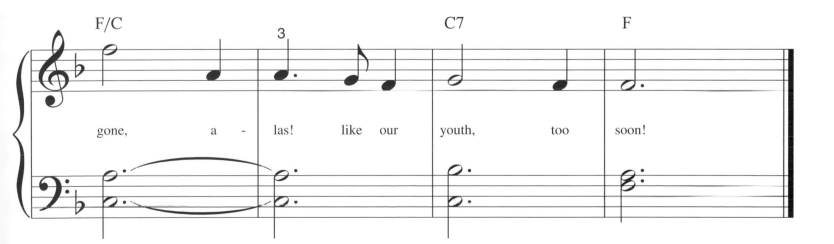

gone, a - las! like our youth, too soon!

A LITTLE BIT OF HEAVEN

Words by ERNEST R. BALL
Music by J. KEIRN BRENAN

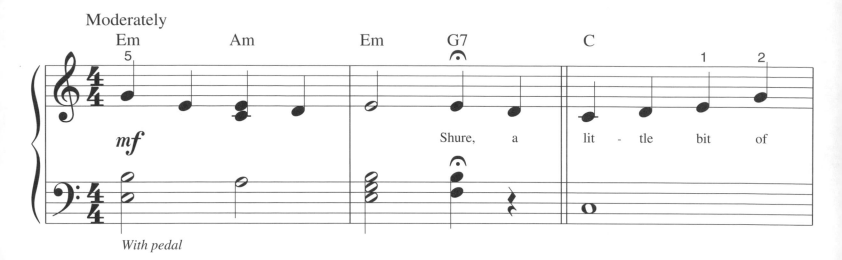

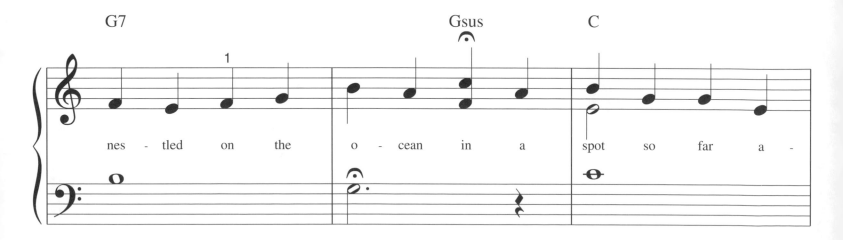

way. And when the an - gels found it, shure it

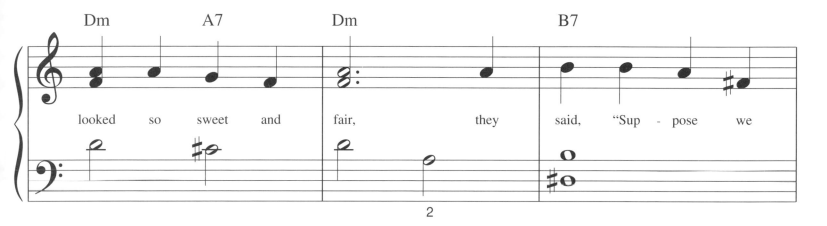

looked so sweet and fair, they said, "Sup - pose we

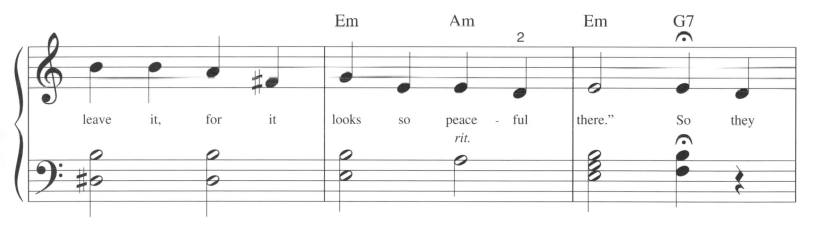

leave it, for it looks so peace - ful there." So they

rit.

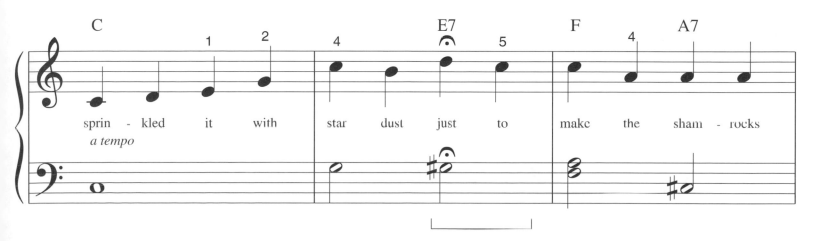

sprin - kled it with star dust just to make the sham - rocks

a tempo

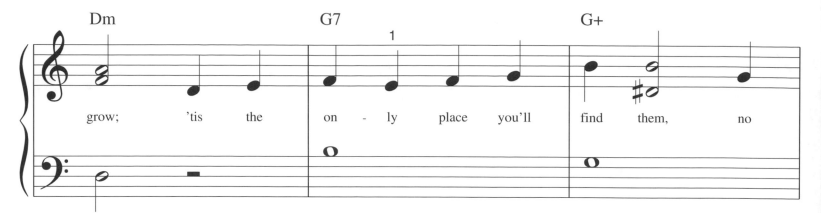

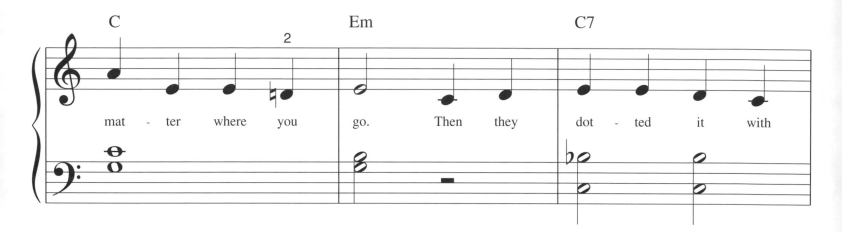

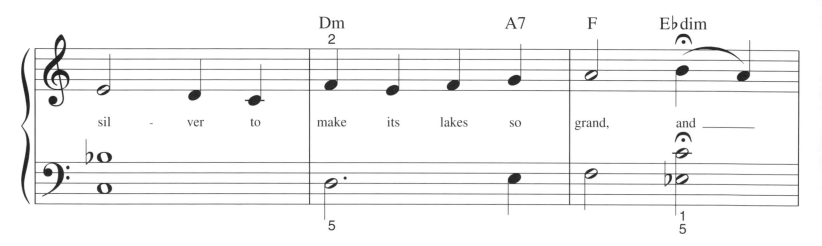

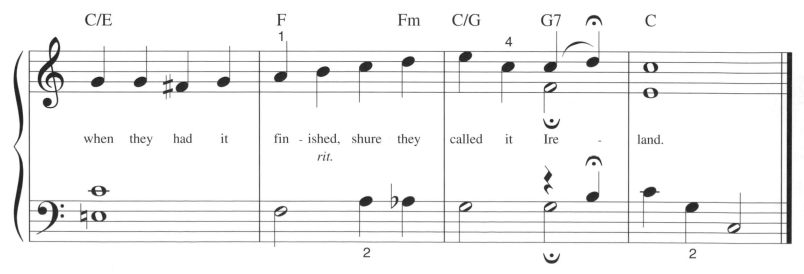

MOLLY MALONE
(Cockles & Mussels)

Irish Folksong

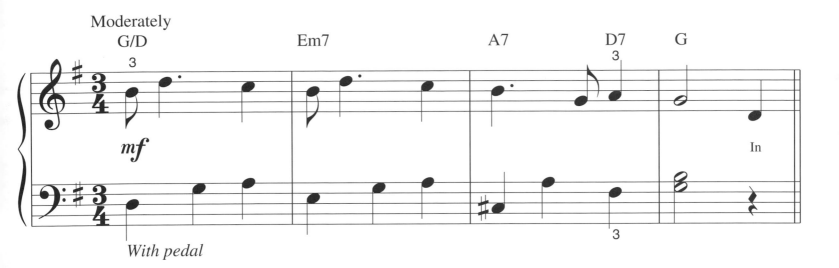

Moderately

With pedal

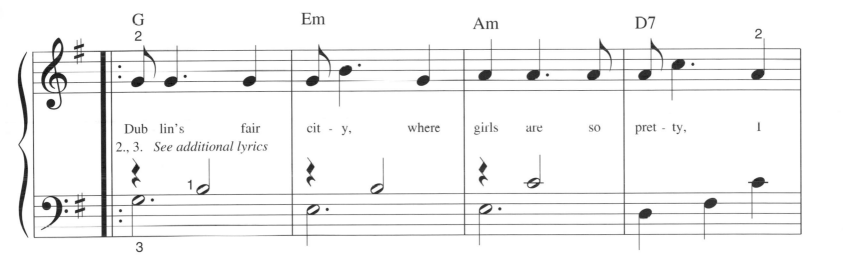

Dub - lin's fair cit - y, where girls are so pret - ty, I
2., 3. *See additional lyrics*

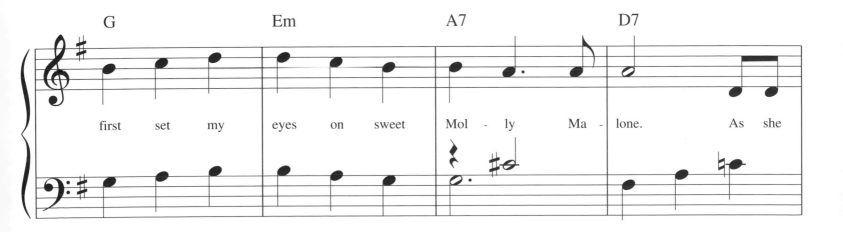

first set my eyes on sweet Mol - ly Ma - lone. As she

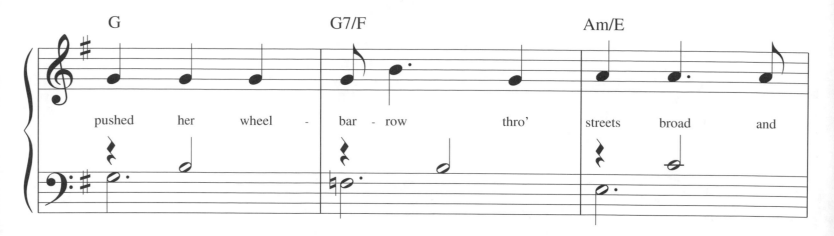

G   G7/F   Am/E

pushed her wheel - bar - row thro' streets broad and

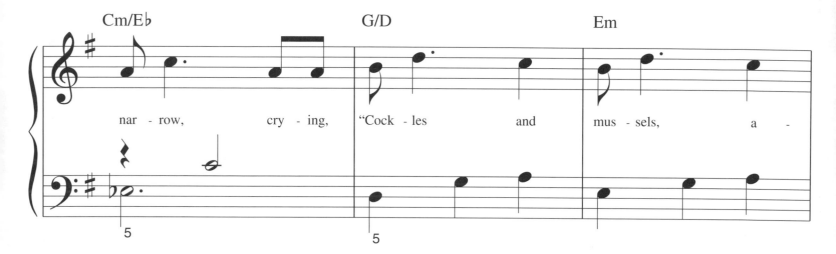

Cm/E♭   G/D   Em

nar - row, cry - ing, "Cock - les and mus - sels, a -

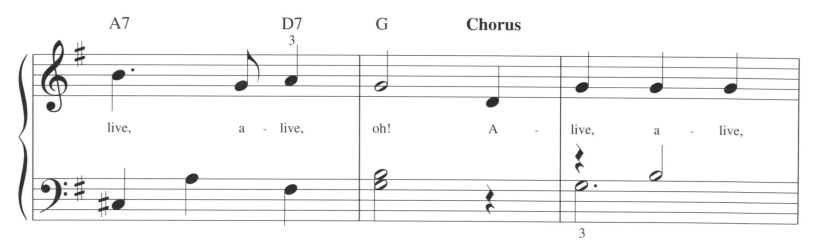

A7   D7   G   **Chorus**

live, a - live, oh! A - live, a - live,

G7/F   Am/E   Cm/E♭

oh! _____ A - live, a - live, oh!" _____ Cry - ing,

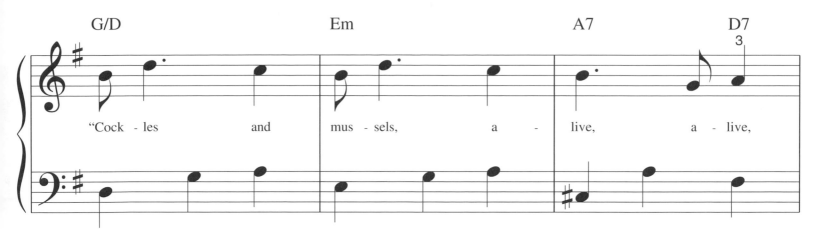

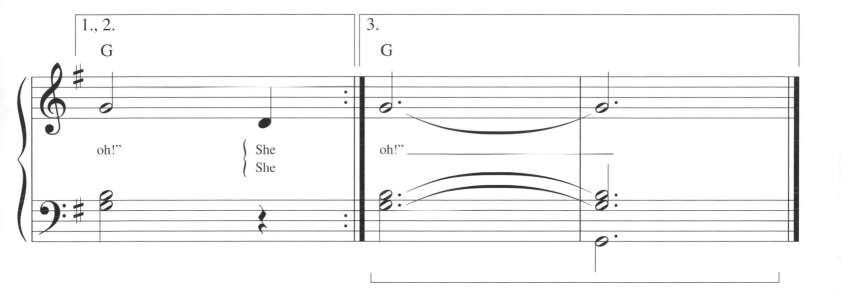

Additional Lyrics

2. She was a fishmonger, but sure 'twas no wonder,
    For so were her father and mother before.
    And they each wheeled their barrow thro' streets broad and narrow,
    Crying, "Cockles and mussels, alive, alive, oh!"
    Chorus

3. She died of a fever and no one could save her,
    And that was the end of sweet Molly Malone.
    But her ghost wheels her barrow thro' streets broad and narrow,
    Crying, "Cockles and mussels, alive, alive, oh!"
    Chorus

MINSTREL BOY

Traditional

With expression

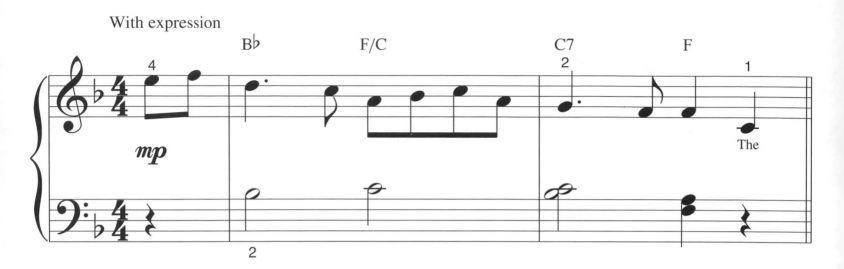

The

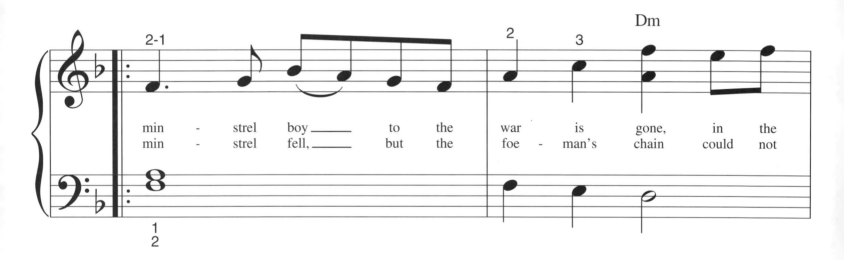

min - strel boy _____ to the war is gone, in the
min - strel fell, _____ but the foe - man's chain could not

ranks of death _____ you'll find _____ him. His fa - ther's sword _ he has
bring his proud _____ soul un - der. The harp he loved _ nev - er

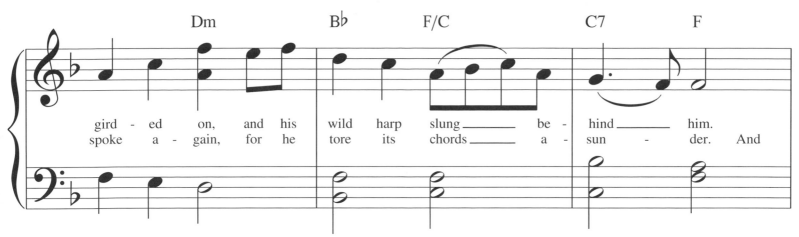

gird - ed on, and his wild harp slung_____ be - hind_____ him.
spoke a - gain, for he tore its chords_____ a - sun - der. And

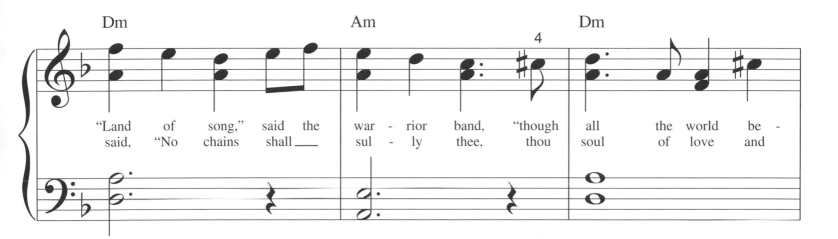

"Land of song," said the war - rior band, "though all the world be -
said, "No chains shall_____ sul - ly thee, thou soul of love and

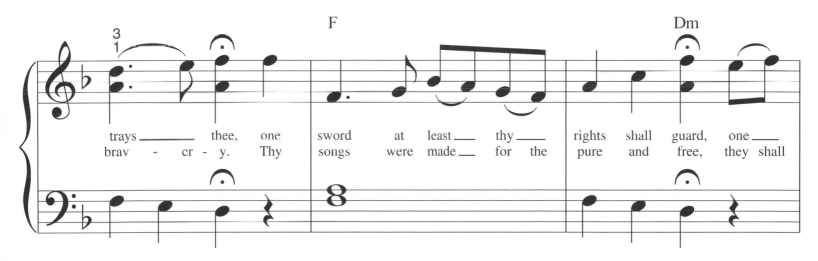

trays_____ thee, one sword at least_____ thy_____ rights shall guard, one_____
brav - er - y. Thy songs were made_____ for the pure and free, they shall

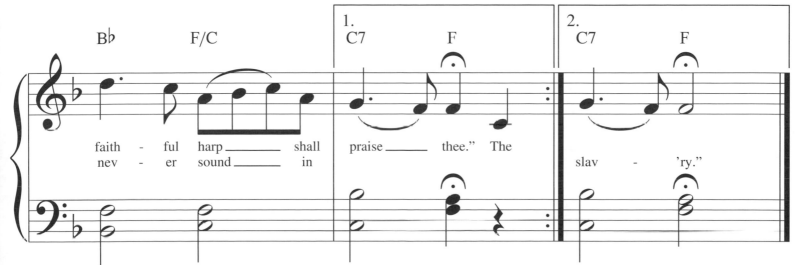

faith - ful harp_____ shall praise_____ thee." The
nev - er sound_____ in slav - 'ry."

MOTHER MACHREE

Words by RIDA JOHNSON YOUNG
Music by CHAUNCEY OLCOTT and ERNEST R. BALL

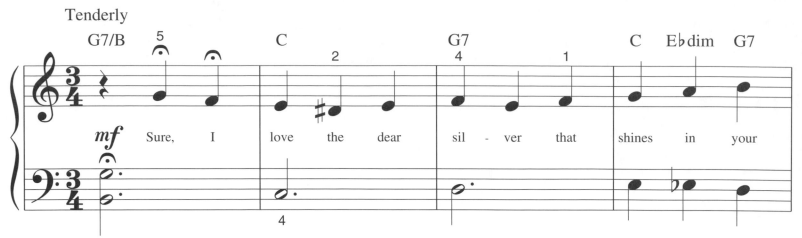

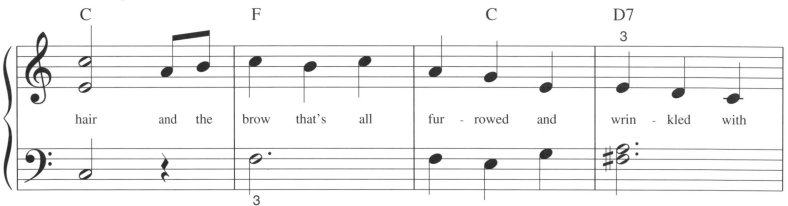

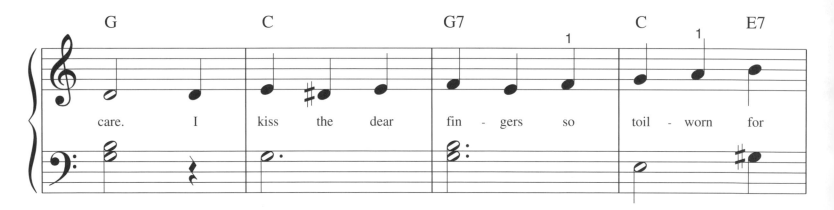

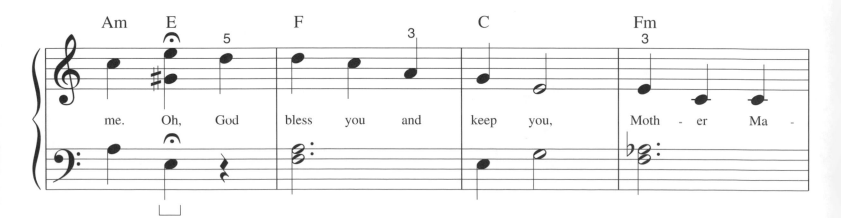

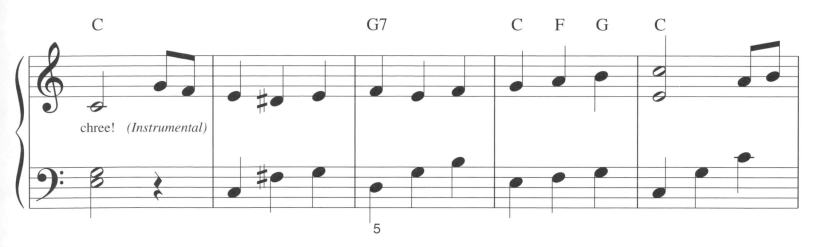

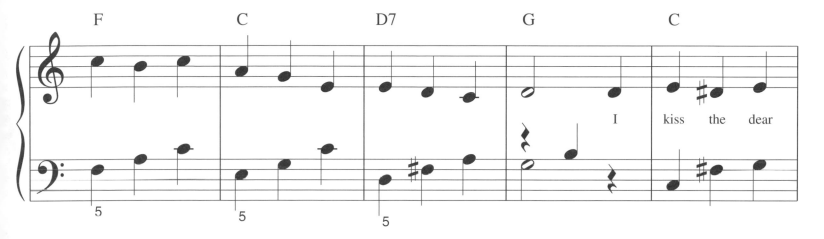

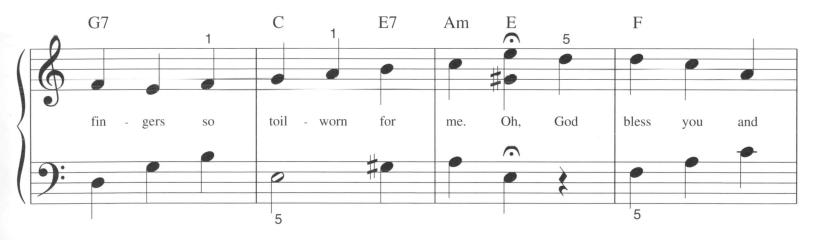

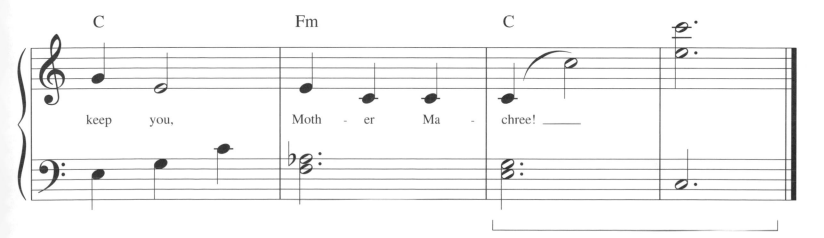

MY WILD IRISH ROSE

Words and Music by
CHAUNCEY OLCOTT

Moderately

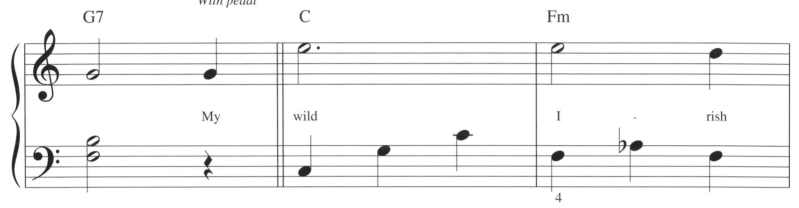

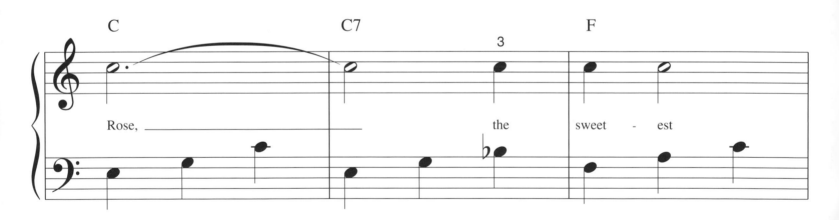

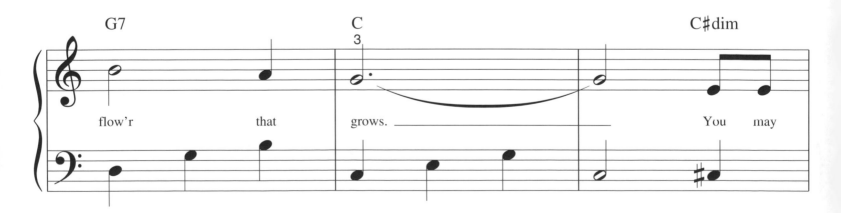

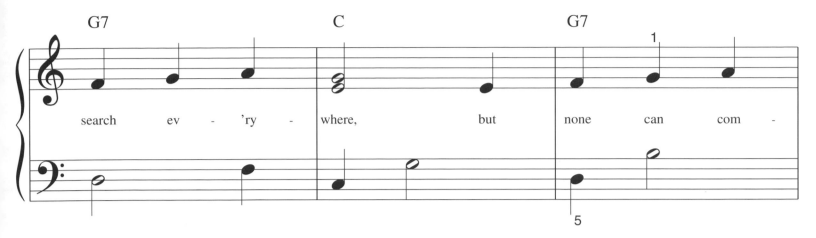

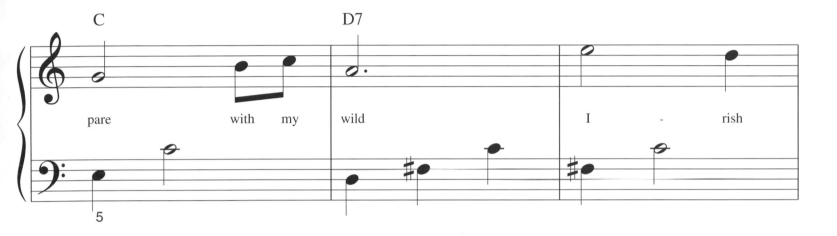

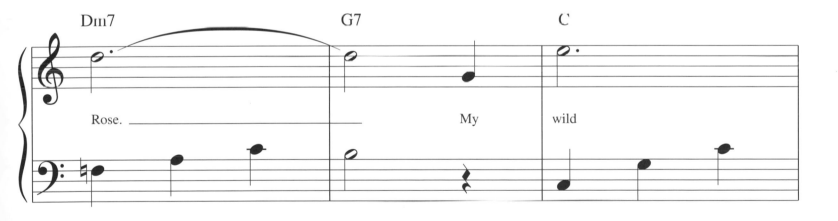

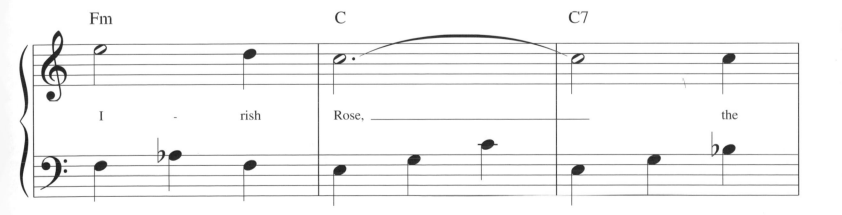

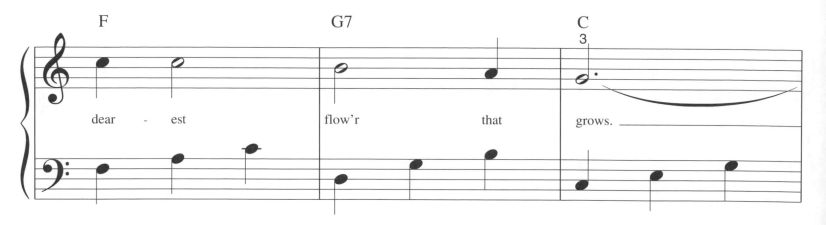

dear - est | flow'r | that | grows. _____

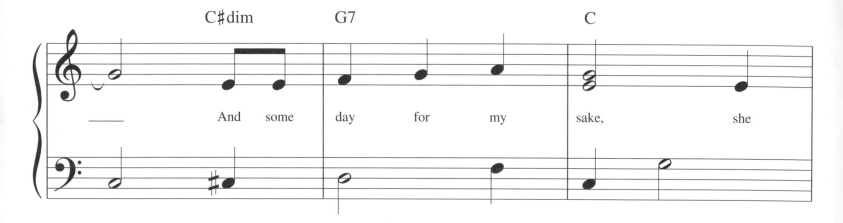

_____ And some | day for my | sake, | she

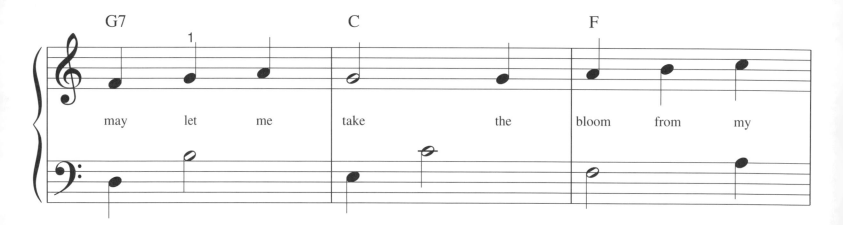

may let me | take | the | bloom from my

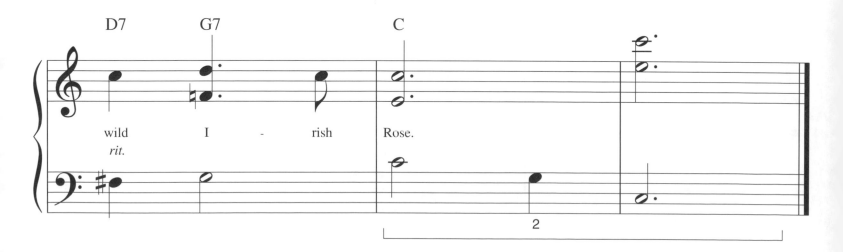

wild I - rish | Rose.

rit.

TOO-RA-LOO-RA-LOO-RAL
(That's an Irish Lullaby)

Words and Music by
JAMES R. SHANNON

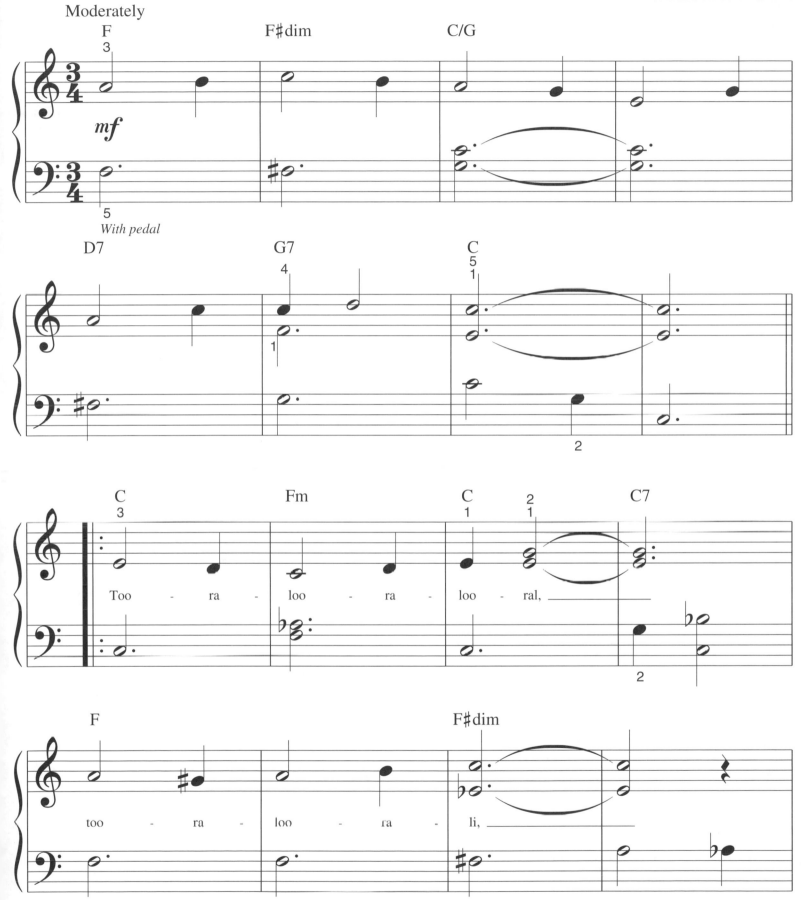

Too - ra - loo - ra - loo - ral,

too - ra - loo - ra - li,

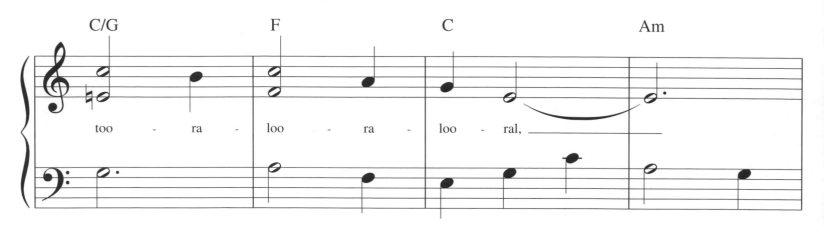

too - ra - loo - ra - loo - ral, _____

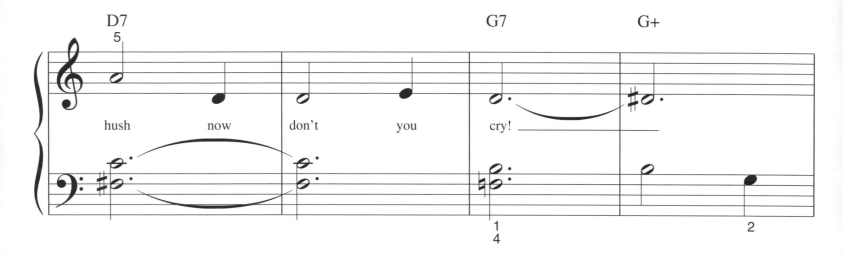

hush now don't you cry!

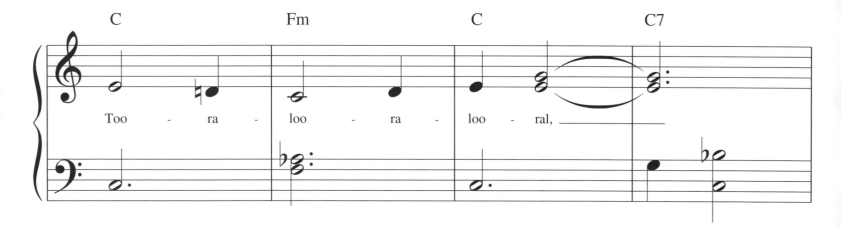

Too - ra - loo - ra - loo - ral, _____

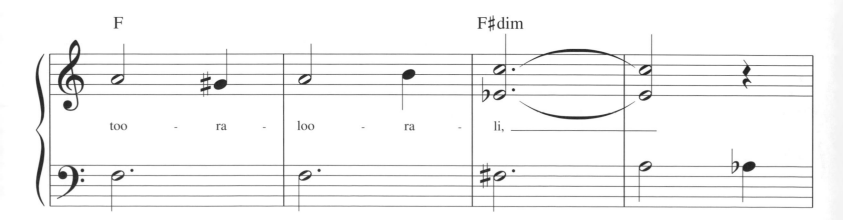

too - ra - loo - ra - li, _____

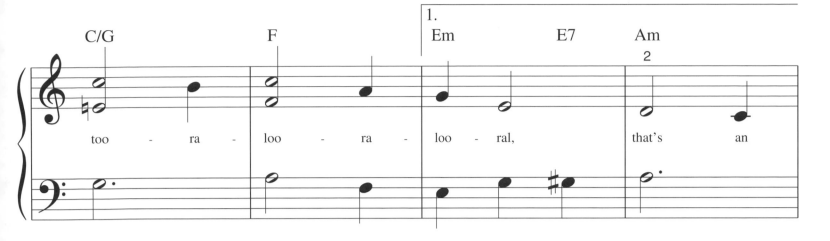

C/G   F   1. Em   E7   Am

too - ra - loo - ra - loo - ral, that's an

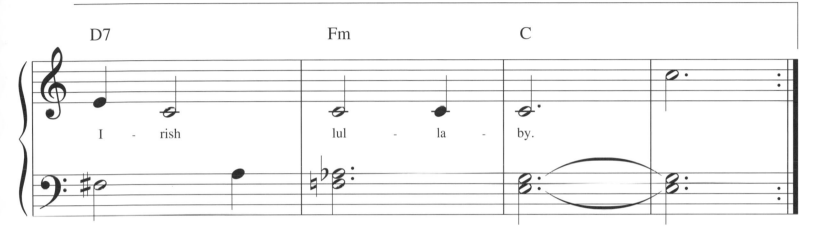

D7   Fm   C

I - rish lul - la - by.

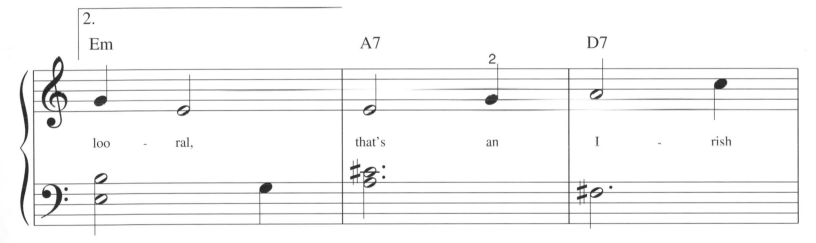

2. Em   A7   D7

loo - ral, that's an I - rish

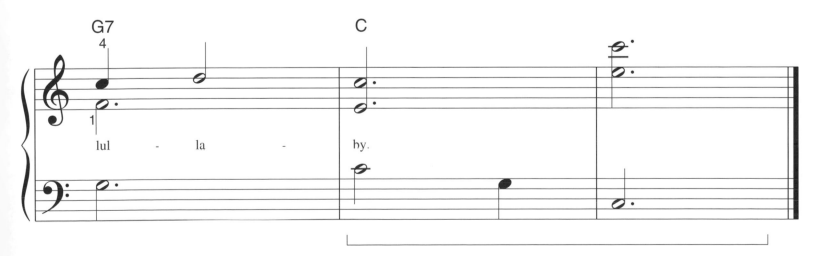

G7   C

lul - la - by.

SWEET ROSIE O'GRADY

Words and Music by
MAUDE NUGENT

Waltz tempo

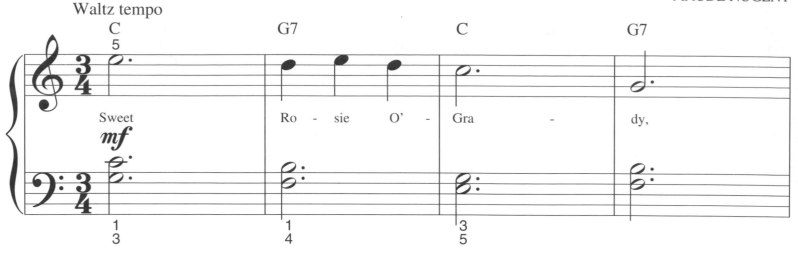

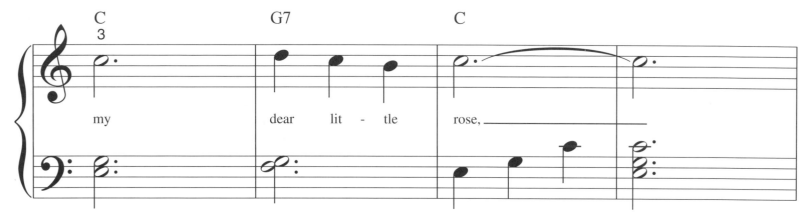

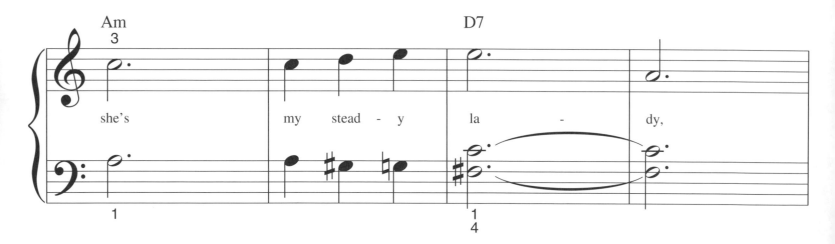

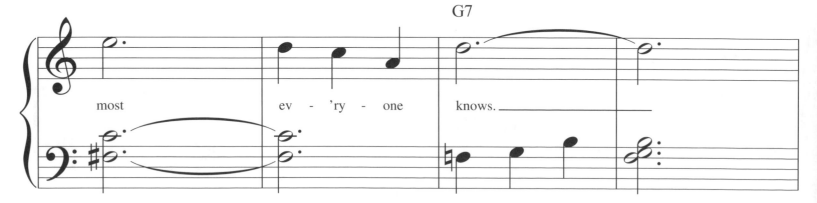

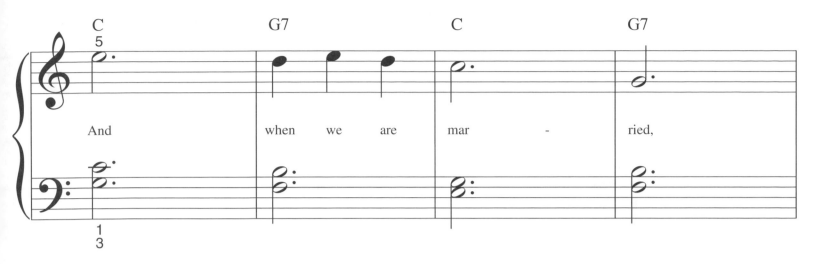

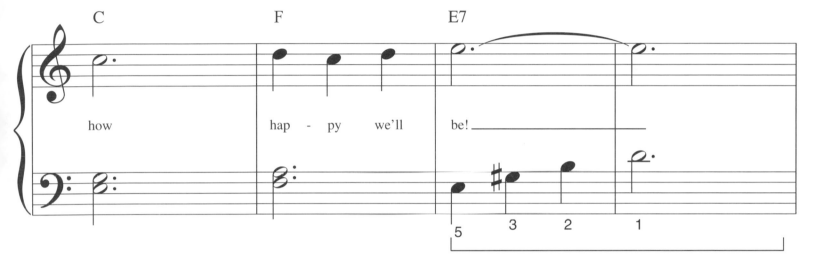

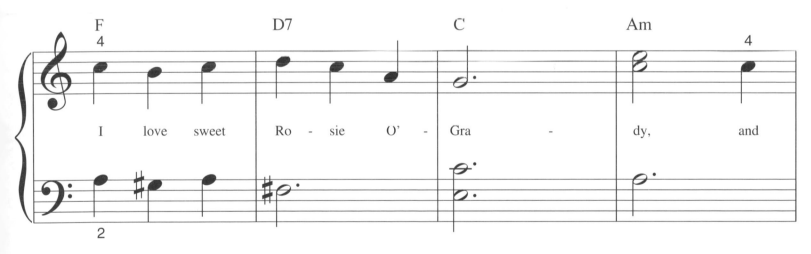

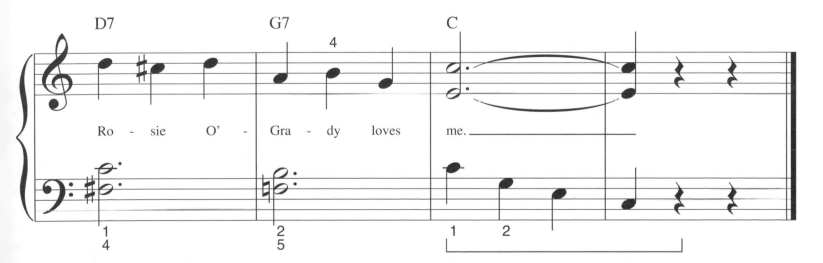

'TIS THE LAST ROSE OF SUMMER

Words by THOMAS MOORE
Music by RICHARD ALFRED MILLIKEN

Slowly and tenderly

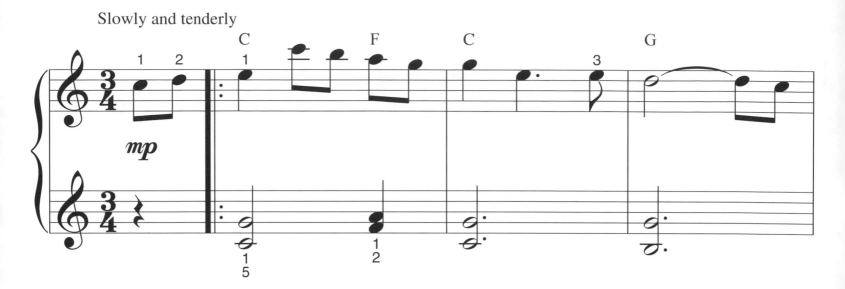

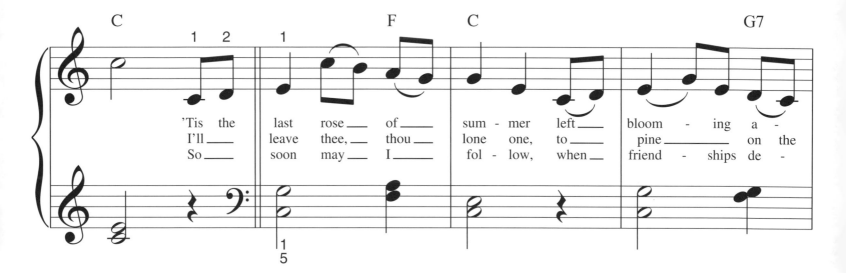

'Tis the last rose __ of __ sum - mer left __ bloom - ing a -
I'll __ leave thee, __ thou __ lone one, to __ pine __ on the
So __ soon may __ I __ fol - low, when __ friend - ships de -

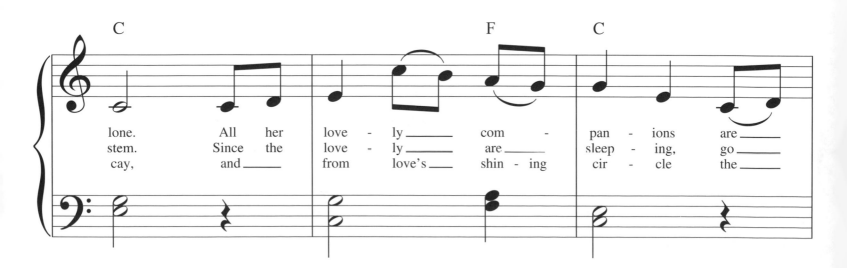

lone. All her love - ly __ com - pan - ions are __
stem. Since the love - ly __ are __ sleep - ing, go __
cay, and __ from love's __ shin - ing cir - cle the __

THE WEARING OF THE GREEN

Eighteenth Century Irish Folksong

Moderately

Oh, ____

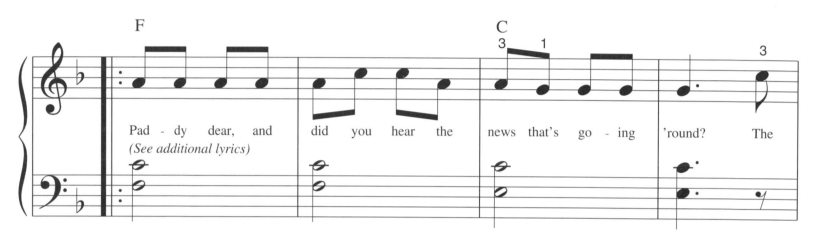

Pad - dy dear, and
(See additional lyrics)
did you hear the news that's go - ing 'round? The

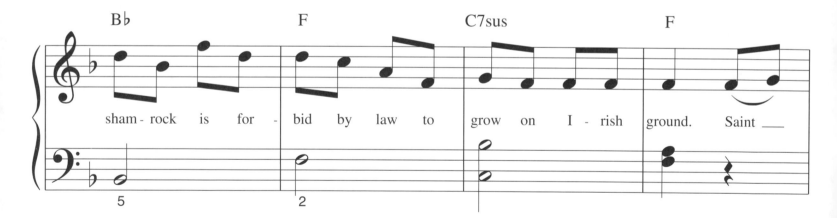

sham - rock is for - bid by law to grow on I - rish ground. Saint ___

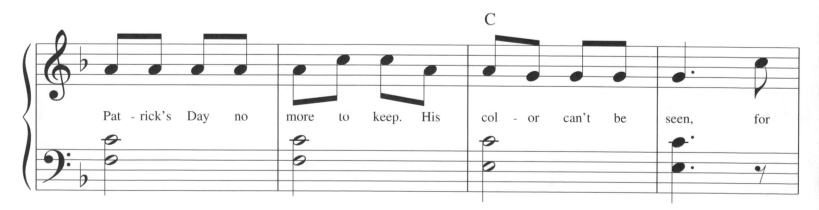

Pat - rick's Day no more to keep. His col - or can't be seen, for

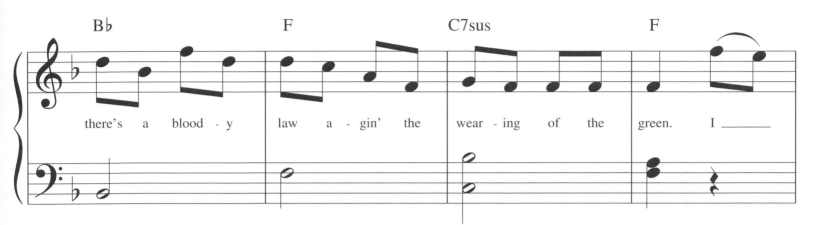

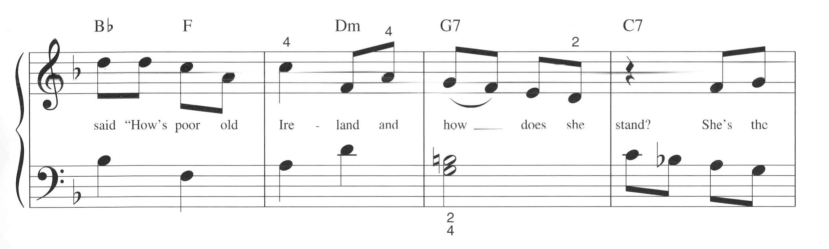

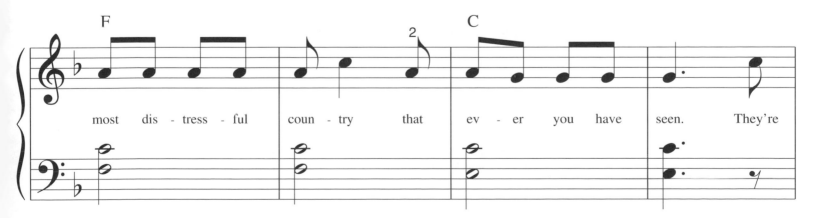

Additional Lyrics

2. Then since the color we must wear is England's cruel red,
   Sure Ireland's sons will ne'er forget the blood that they have shed.
   You may take the shamrock from your hat and cast it on the sod,
   But 'twill take root and flourish still, though under foot it's trod.
   When the law can stop the blades of grass from growing as they grow
   And when the leaves in summertime their verdure dare not show,
   Then I will change the color that I wear in my corbeen.
   But till that day, please God, I'll stick to wearing of the green.

3. But, if at last our color should be torn from Ireland's heart,
   Her sons, with shame and sorrow, from the dear old sail will part.
   I've heard whisper of a country that lies far beyond the sea
   Where rich and poor stand equal in the light of freedom's day.
   Oh, Erin, must we leave you, driven by the tyrant's hand?
   Must we ask a mother's welcome from a strange, but happier land?
   Where the cruel cross of England's thraldom never shall be seen,
   And where, thank God, we'll live and die still wearing of the green.

WHEN IRISH EYES ARE SMILING

Words by CHAUNCEY OLCOTT and GEORGE GRAFF, Jr.
Music by ERNEST R. BALL

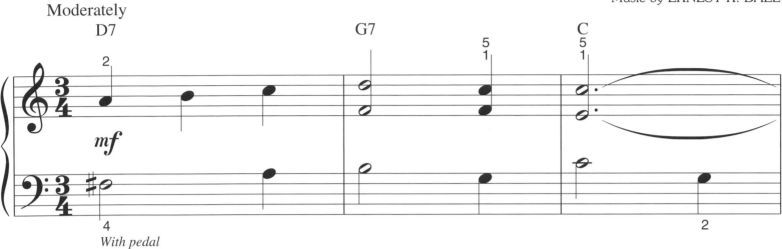

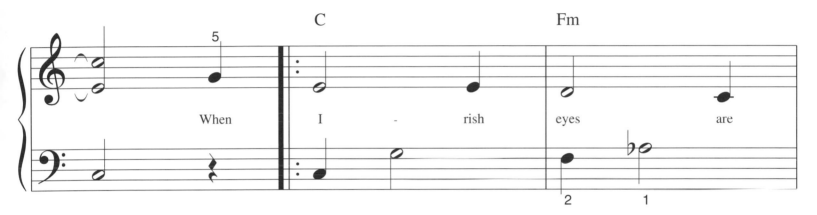

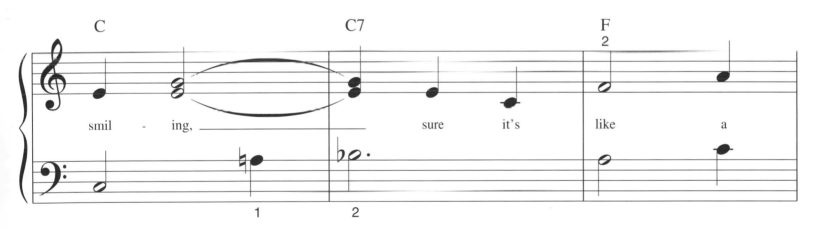

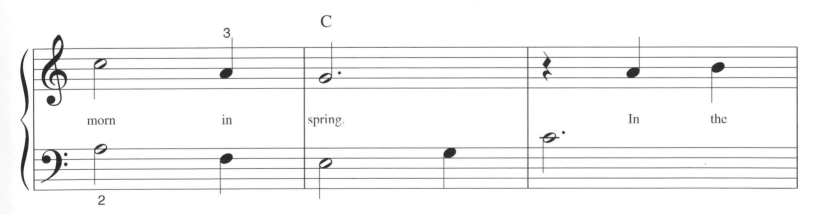

56

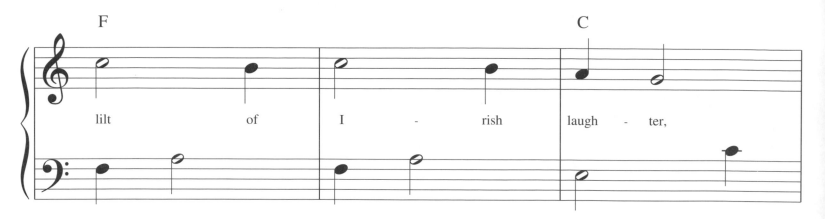

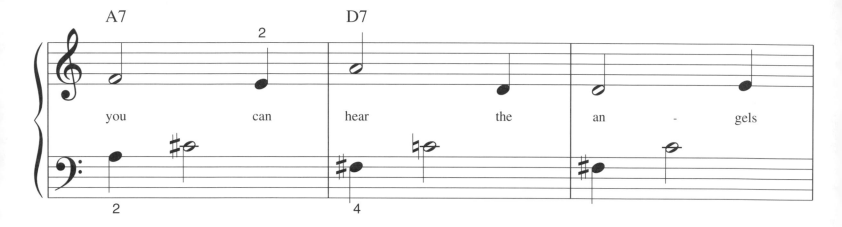

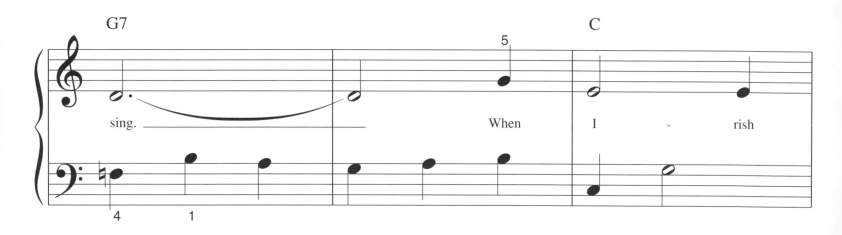

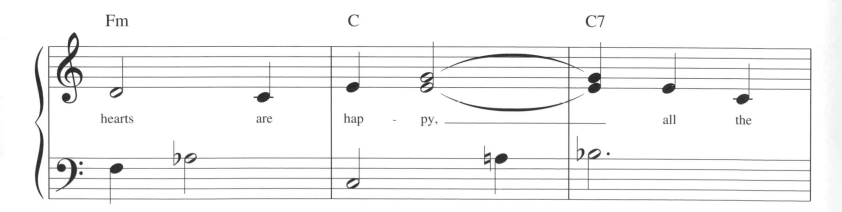

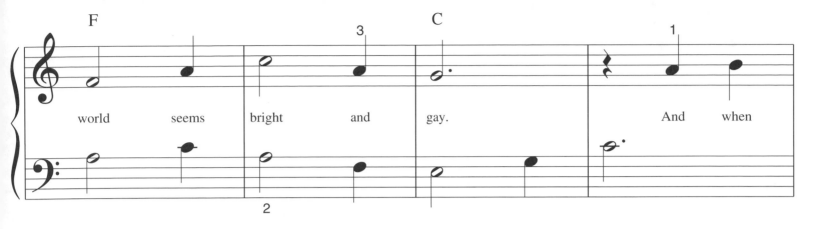

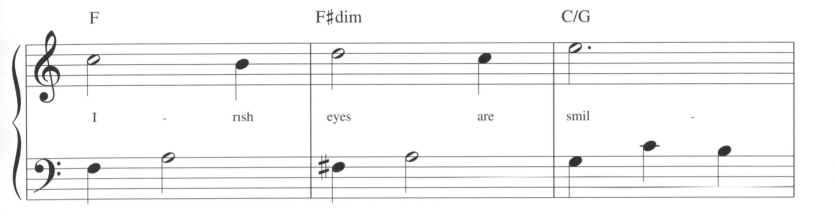

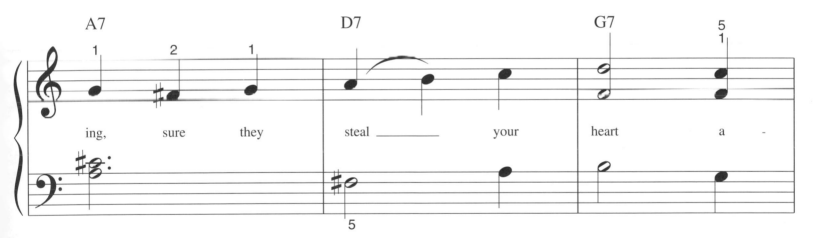

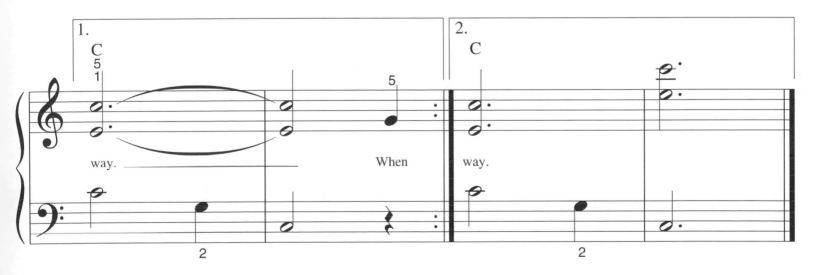

WHO THREW THE OVERALLS IN MRS. MURPHY'S CHOWDER

Words and Music by
GEORGE L. GIEFER

Moderately

Mis - tress

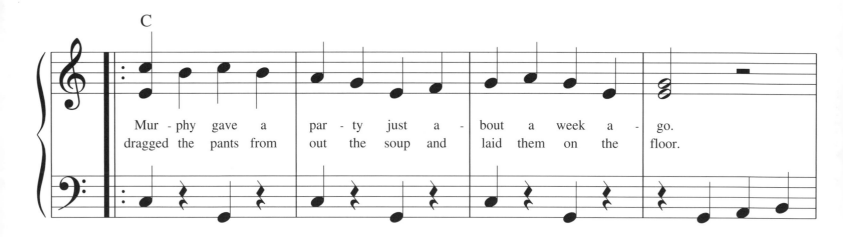

Mur - phy gave a par - ty just a - bout a week a - go.
dragged the pants from out the soup and laid them on the floor.

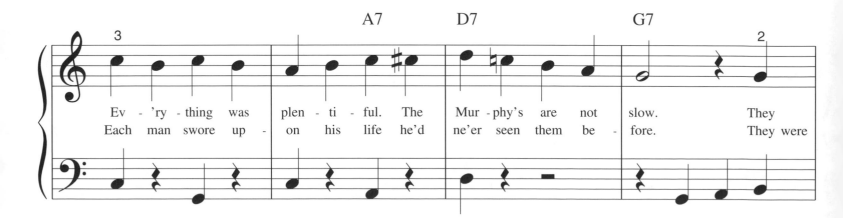

Ev - 'ry - thing was plen - ti - ful. The Mur - phy's are not slow. They
Each man swore up - on his life he'd ne'er seen them be - fore. They were

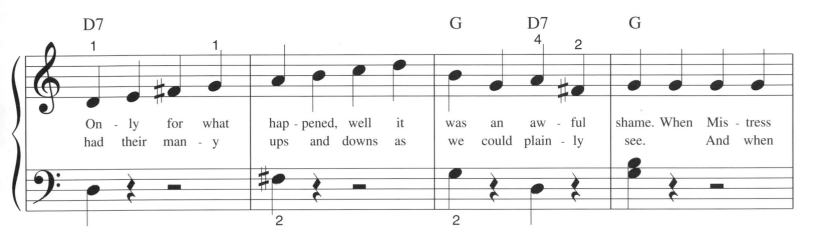

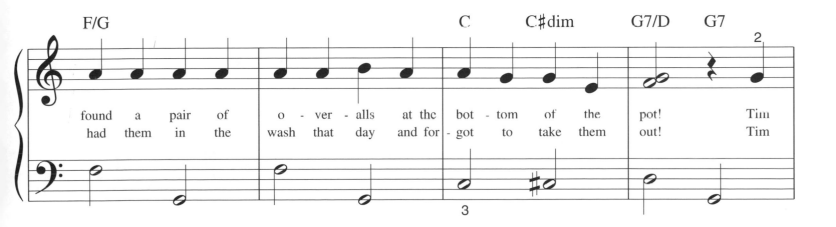

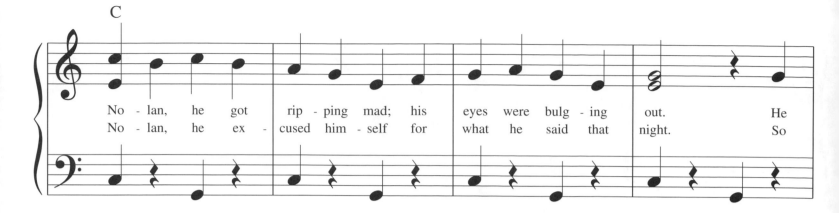

No - lan, he got rip - ping mad; his eyes were bulg - ing out. He
No - lan, he ex - cused him - self for what he said that night. So

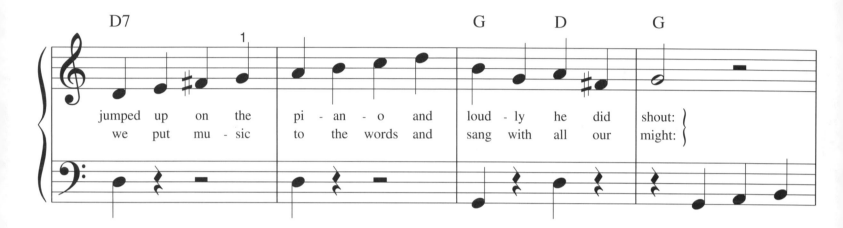

jumped up on the pi - an - o and loud - ly he did shout:
we put mu - sic to the words and sang with all our might:

"Who threw the o - ver - alls in Mis - tress Mur - phy's chow - der?"

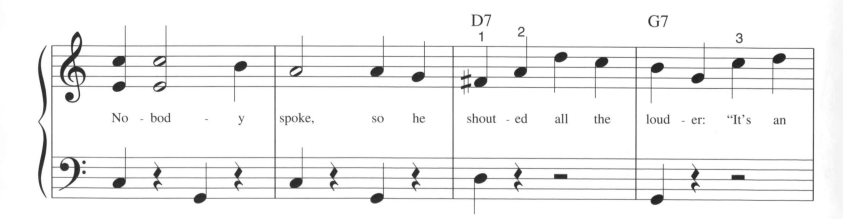

No - bod - y spoke, so he shout - ed all the loud - er: "It's an

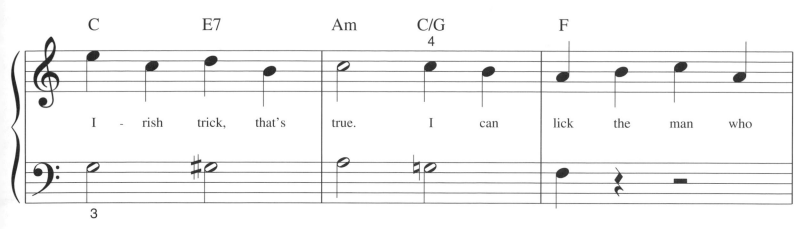

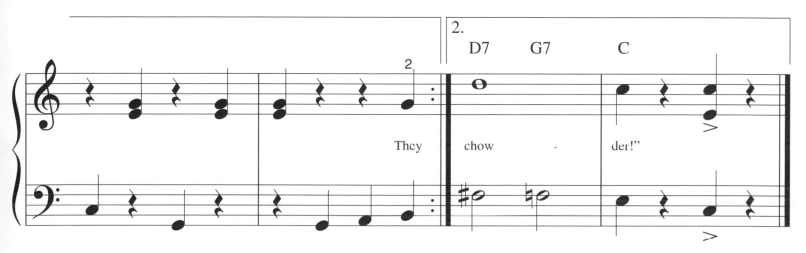

WHERE THE RIVER SHANNON FLOWS

By JAMES J. RUSSELL

Moderately

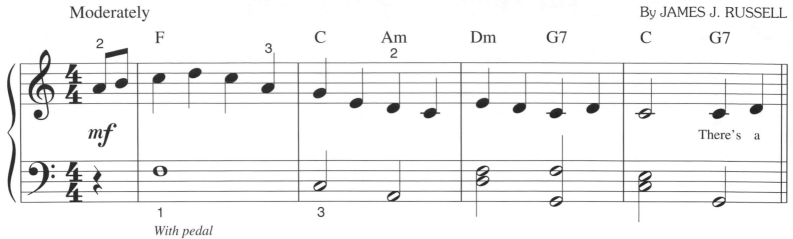

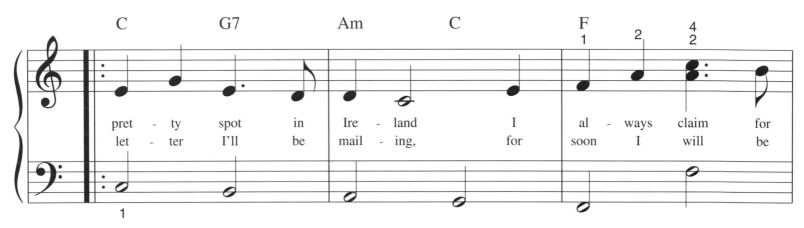

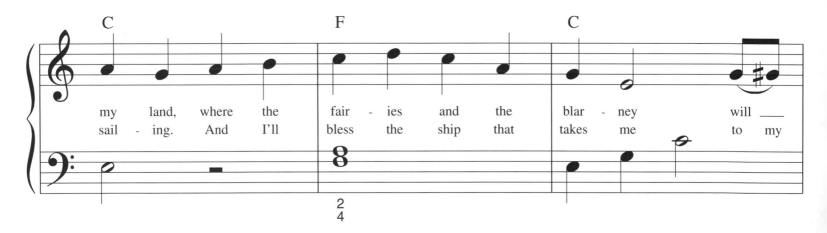

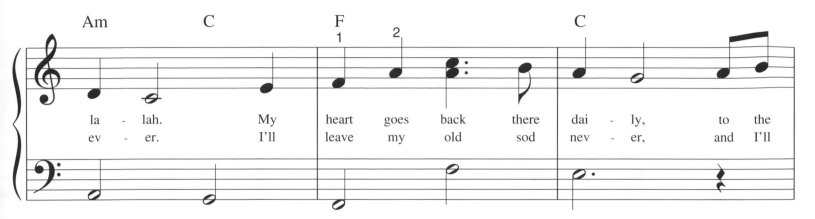

la - lah.   My | heart goes back there dai - ly,   to the
ev - er.   I'll | leave my old sod nev - er,   and I'll

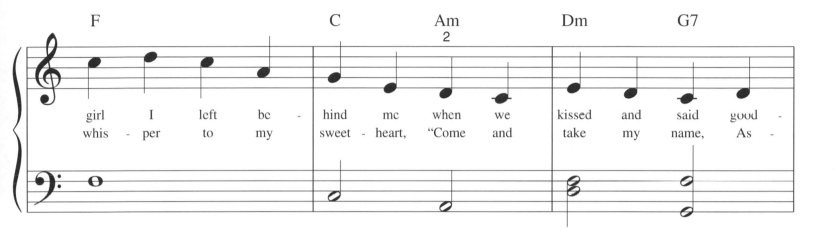

girl I left be - | hind me when we | kissed and said good -
whis - per to my | sweet - heart, "Come and | take my name, As -

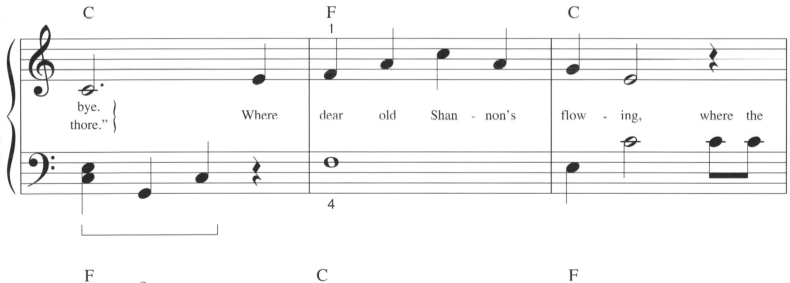

bye.
thore." } | Where dear old Shan - non's | flow - ing,   where the

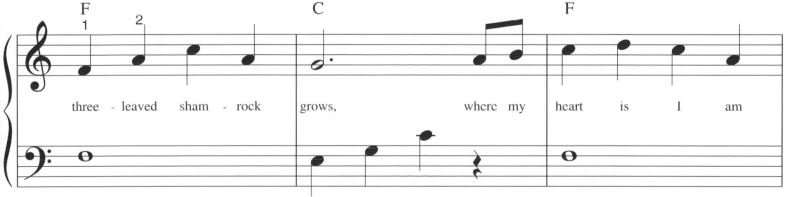

three - leaved sham - rock | grows,   where my | heart is I am

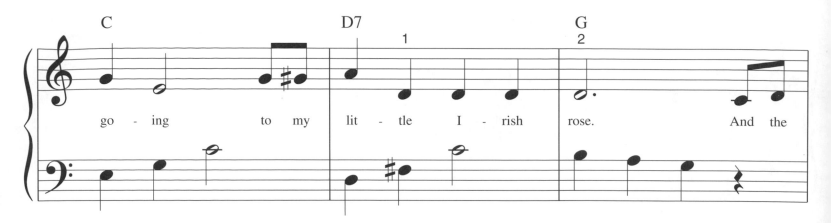

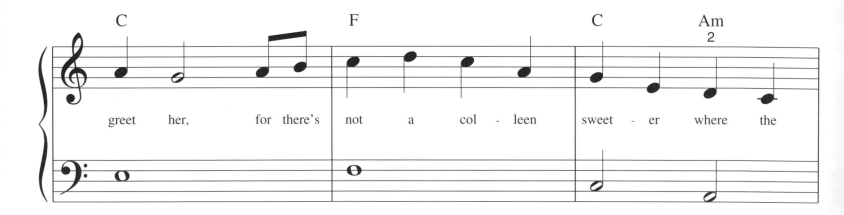

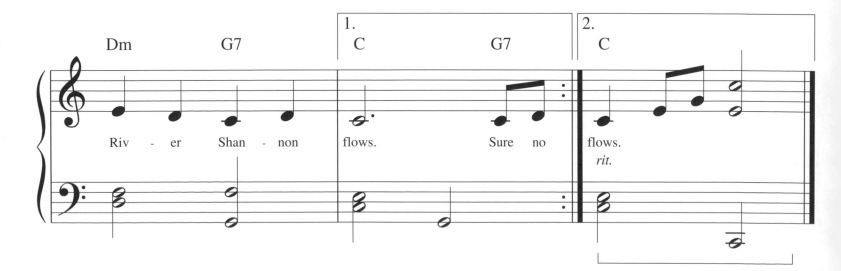